WHAT CAN A PARENT DO?

Handbook for the *Fives to Fifteens* Parenting Programme

Michael & Terri Quinn

FAMILY CARING TRUST

First published 1986
by Veritas Family Resources,
7/8 Lower Abbey Street,
Dublin 1.

Published 1987
by Family Caring Trust,
8 Ashtree Enterprise Park
Newry Co. Down BT34 1BY

Revised edition published 1988, 1989, 1990 (twice), 1991, 1992,
1993, 1994 (twice), 1995, 1996, 1997, 1998, 1999

New revised 21st century edition October 2000
Reprinted 2002, 2003

Design: Bill Bolger
Illustrations: John Byrne and Pauline McGrath
Printing: Universities Press (Belfast)

ISBN 1 872253 17 2

CONTENTS

FAMILY CARING TRUST

IS PARTICULARLY GRATEFUL TO

Barnardos

FOR THEIR GENEROUS CONTRIBUTION

TOWARDS THE DEVELOPMENT AND PRODUCTION

OF THIS BOOK AND PROGRAMME

CHILDREN HAVE RIGHTS

The UN Convention on the Rights of the Child is the first document to attempt to write down all the rights of children. Here are some highlights – and some corresponding rights of parents. It may be more helpful to replace 'right to' with 'need (for)' and to think of these rights as basic needs.

1. Children have a right to be respected by their parents or guardians, and to be involved in decisions that affect themselves.
2. Children have a right to say what they want and think and feel so long as doing so does not break the law or affect other people's rights.
3. Children have a right to personal privacy, including not having personal letters opened or phone calls listened to unless the law allows this.
4. Children have a right to a wide range of information, especially any which would make life better for them.
5. Children have a right to proper care and protection from all forms of violence, including cruel punishment, belittling, or lack of respect.
6. Children have a right to an adequate standard of living, good food, good health care, and the best possible chance to develop fully.
7. Disabled children have a right to be enabled to take an active, full part in everyday life and become as autonomous as possible.
8. Every child is entitled to rest and play, and to have the chance to join in a wide range of activities.

...AND PARENTS HAVE RIGHTS

1. Parents have the same right to be listened to and respected by their children as their children have to be listened to and respected by their parents.
2. Parents have a right to time for relaxing and developing themselves – also a right to time on their own with a spouse or other significant adult.
3. Parents have a right to postpone making a decision until they have had time to think.
4. Parents have a right to say 'no,' to set reasonable limits for their children, and, within reason, to let them live with the results of ignoring those limits.
5. Parents have a right to have their work at home valued and appreciated by the significant people in their lives as well as by government and state bodies.
6. Parents have the right to ask their children for reasonable help around the home, according to each child's ability.
7. Parents have a right to communicate their values and opinions to their children – though they cannot insist on their children having the same values.
8. Parents have a right to proper support in providing their children with due rights and respect.

Do you agree that you and your children have these rights? Which of your children's rights might you find hardest to respect? Which of your own rights might you find hardest to claim?

BEFORE YOU BEGIN...

Finding Support

This book is part of an eight-week parenting programme, which includes a video and a Leader's guide. Parents find the book useful on its own, but it may be best to read it a little at a time as parents do during a course. And it will be useful if you can talk with other parents about the ideas. Their support can help lessen any sense of parenting on your own – or of guilt about not being a perfect parent!

You do not need more guilt. It is pointless to blame yourself for anything you were not aware of or capable of in the past. Besides, there is no such thing as a perfect parent, and that is certainly not the ideal offered in this book. We suggest you settle for being 'good enough.' That can be an important starting point on the road to being more effective. If you do suffer from guilt – or from the effects of neglect or abuse when you were a child – maybe the very best thing you can do for your parenting is to find a wise counsellor or a good friend who can listen well and offer you the support you need.

If you are interested in belonging to a parenting group, you may like to contact your school, health visitor, church, or a local organisation that is interested in family life. Family Caring Trust provides materials and ongoing support to thousands of such groups.

Using what works for you.

Everyone is different. What works with one child will not necessarily work with another. So much depends on your own circumstances, on the position of a child in your family – even on your mood. There is no suggestion, then, that the ideas in this book will suit everyone. It is good to *hear* other people's ideas, but it is your children who really teach you about parenting, and no one knows them as you do. It does not help to let experts dictate to you or tell you how to parent. We suggest you try out new ideas in order to see if they might work better for you, but feel free to reject or disagree with anything in these pages.

Some examples may seem unusual or extreme – like allowing your daughter to be late for school. But it is important to see an example like this in context. If you are wearing yourself out every morning coaxing and nagging at a child who lies on in bed, it may help to give her an alarm clock and allow her to face the consequences of being late for school. Use what works for you.

The examples in the book are taken from different family situations and social backgrounds. In one family, problems may arise over pocket money; other parents may not give their children pocket money at all. In one family there may be tension over a teenager's careless driving of the parents' car. Another family may not be able to afford a car, and they may be experiencing acute problems because of unemployment. A third family's problems may arise from the difficulties of bringing up children as a single parent. When parents see how the principles of the course apply in a few situations, it is usually not difficult to apply them in their own families.

Who is it for?

This book is for grandparents, foster-parents and child-carers as well as for ordinary parents, including those who are single or separated, those whose families are broken or mixed and those who are happily married. It is written in simple language – though a number of new terms are introduced and explained at different stages. Many good ideas could have been included but were left out in order to keep the book simple and practical; people generally prefer to deal with just one new idea at a time. Most parents probably do not need very special knowledge of child psychology and the development of children. It is enough if they have some basic understanding of and love for their children – and some skills.

Parents of teenagers tend to find this book as useful as do parents of younger children. The challenges of an adolescent may be quite different to those of a younger child, but the skills for dealing with them are similar. Our 'Parenting Teenagers' Programme has been specially developed, however, for parents of teenagers who have followed this course and then wish to move on to look at more specific teenage challenges.

Beliefs and influences

It may be important, right from the start, to acknowledge some of the beliefs and influences affecting our own ideas on bringing up children. We believe in a balanced approach that is neither rigidly authoritarian nor overly permissive. We want to foster greater respect in families and in society by respecting and fostering children's rights and by respecting and fostering parents' rights. We would like to help parents appreciate their leadership role in a family, guiding, listening, supporting, setting an example, stimulating, challenging, affectionate but firm, generally creating an environment in which children can learn to love and be responsible and develop to their fullest potential.

Our aim in this programme is not to change or modify children's behaviour to come up to some kind of ideal or model. Each child is a unique and special person, and part of a parent's role is not only to encourage responsibility and co-operation but also to protect and nurture a child's own creativity and uniqueness.

Acknowledgements

There is little that is original in the book. We owe a great deal to the ideas of Alfred Adler, Steve Biddulph, Don Dinkmeyer, Rudolf Dreikurs, Gerard Egan, Haim Ginnott, Thomas Gordon, John Gottman, Harvey Jackins, Gary McKay, Carl Rogers, Virginia Satir and Ron Taffel. We also owe much to a number of parenting programmes, notably 'Systematic Training for Effective Parenting;' 'Parent Effectiveness Training,' and 'Practical Parenting.' If you would like more information about our value base you might visit our website at www.familycaring.co.uk – and there is a recommended reading list at the back of this book.

We would like to say a special word of thanks to all the people who helped to test this programme throughout Britain and Ireland, in rural and city communities, in multi-racial groups and under-privileged areas as well as with professional people. We have been impressed that people of every walk of life seem to find common cause and speak a common language when faced with basic parenting situations.

We are especially grateful to our own children to whom we owe so much. They have challenged us and stretched us and forced us to grow – and to learn to love a little more. And they have given us lots of laughs and friendship and good times too!

for ordinary parents...

CHAPTER 1: WHAT IS YOUR CHILD LOOKING FOR?

Jane: Mummy, Peter thumped me!
Mrs Stewart: Peter! *(pause)* Peter!!
Peter: What's wrong?
Mrs Stewart: Why did you thump Jane?
Peter: I didn't thump her. She was annoying me, and I pushed her away.
Jane: No, Mummy. I was watching TV and he came in and switched it over to something *he* wanted to see, then he thumped me when I tried to switch it back.
Peter: I didn't thump you, crybaby! I switched over because I always watch that programme. And you know it, you little b..!
Mrs Stewart: I won't have you using that language in this house, Peter! And I don't know how often I've spoken to you about bullying. I'll kill you one of these days if you don't stop it!
Peter: Sure, blame me! I always get the blame. But little 'angel-face' never does anything wrong! Well, I'm just fed-up with all the blame! *(Peter goes out, and slams the door.)*
Mrs Stewart: *(rushes to door)* Peter! Come back in here again, and walk out through this door properly! That's no way to treat...

How we take the bait

This kind of scene is not uncommon in many families. Squabbling among children is disheartening and upsetting for many parents, and we are often at a loss to know what to do.

But what do you think of the way Mrs Stewart was handling the situation? She is not being very effective, is she? The squabbling, bullying and tattling are obviously problems that keep cropping up again and again in her family. And did you notice how she took the bait? – first Jane's, and then Peter's. Her children probably know exactly what she's going to say, for she keeps letting herself get drawn into blaming, scolding, making empty threats, and attempting to correct on the spot. She is doing her best to be a good parent, but she tends to act in a fixed, patterned, unthinking – and ineffective – way.

Most children know exactly how to get their parents' attention. They are experts at drawing us into their problems and their squabbles. It's like pressing a button – they can get us to nag, coax, scold, lecture, shout, threaten, hit – even to look for their lost belongings and do things for them that they are quite capable of doing for themselves! **Again and again on a daily basis many parents take their children's bait and get hooked into situations like the one above! They *reward* their children's misbehaviour, even reinforce it, by paying so much attention to it.** Even if the misbehaviour stops for a few minutes, it is almost certain to start again the next time the child wants attention – as long as we parents do just what our children *expect* us to do.

Why do children misbehave?
But why do children misbehave in the first place? What exactly are they seeking? (By misbehaviour we mean any behaviour with which they do not respect themselves or you or others.)

Children usually misbehave because they feel discouraged and bad about themselves. That is not surprising when you think of how much they have to learn and accomplish in the first few years of their lives. When they feel discouraged at not achieving something, they fall back, frustrated, to an earlier stage and seek help in the only way they know – they express their fear, loneliness, worry and discouragement in 'troublesome' behaviour. Here are five common ways in which this behaviour is expressed:
1. Attention-seeking (keeping people busy with them).
2. Power contests (trying to run things).
3. Revenge (trying to hurt people).
4. Showing inadequacy (giving up).
5. Seeking the approval of friends (closely linked to attention-seeking.)

Let's look at some examples of these five ways, and how parents might begin to deal with them.

Attention-seeking
Eight-year-old Nick gets attention by eating slowly. When his mother says, "Come on, now, eat up, Nick," he takes another bite, then slows down again. Mother is giving him the attention he is looking for!

Children need your attention. They need it so desperately that they prefer to be punished or scolded or to do without food rather than be ignored. But the best attention you can give is the attention they do *not* expect rather than attention that they are demanding. Notice what happens when you give them attention on demand – the behaviour that annoys you may stop for a while, but it is likely to continue again soon – or your child starts to misbehave in another way. If you are correcting your five-year-old son again and again for using swear words, you are rewarding his misbehaviour by paying attention to it and the swearing is unlikely to stop.

Misbehaviour is much more likely to stop when it is ignored. So it is not helpful to do what a misbehaving child *expects* you to do. Instead of trying to 'cheer up' a sulking child, you might say, "I'd like to help you, so when you decide what you want, come and talk to me." When your daughter is forever moaning and whinging, you insist on her speaking in a normal voice and refuse to listen until she does. Similarly, instead of coaxing Nick (above) to eat, his mother might withdraw attention from the food, clear his plate at the end of the meal but let him go hungry until the next meal.

I didn't thump you, crybaby...

What is terribly important, however, is to give him the *good* attention he needs – listening, chatting, fun – when he is *not* expecting it. **All children need daily doses of affection, listening, hugs... When they get that, many attention-seeking problems just go away.**

Power contests

Ten-year-old Mary reacts impatiently to her parents and answers them back a lot. When her father argues back or scolds her, there are angry scenes and the whole atmosphere of the house is affected.

This is probably a power struggle. When children get into a power struggle, they often ignore a correction – or get worse when corrected. Even when they give in, they may remain defiant. Behind it all, they are usually searching for limits, needing you to engage with them in order to find security in your boundaries.

We can easily forget that our goal is not to win power contests, for 'winning' often makes matters worse in the long run. So Mary's father needs to **refuse to get involved in the power struggle**. Instead, he might leave the room saying: "We'll talk about this later, Mary, when we're both calmer." (In chapter five we will see how to be more effective in talking things out, but it is important to *remember* to talk later!)

_____

When I stopped interfering in the fights, the children couldn't cope with me and the screaming actually got worse for a while, they were so desperate to draw me into it all. But that's one of the things I've got out of this course – to ignore the squabbles. I was wearing myself out being the judge, asking who hit who first and who said what, and why did she do that, and so on. Now I realise they had become expert at getting my attention with their screams and tattling on one another. I just tell them I trust them to sort it out themselves now and it works most of the time.

_____

Revenge

Thirteen-year-old Liz punishes her parents by constantly complaining about 'this rotten food.' When she is forbidden to speak like that, she gets back at her parents by muttering under her breath and making mealtimes a kind of torture for them. Without even realising it, she may be seeking revenge.

When parents win power struggles regularly, the children may seek revenge by finding ways to hurt and punish them. If you hit back, scold or nag, the child usually changes tactics and finds a new way to hurt you.

It takes patience not to fight back. If you remain friendly, however, you'll soon take the bitterness out of the 'war.' In this case, it may help to acknowledge calmly that Liz does not like the food and ask her to leave the table if she does not want to eat it – then you might change the subject.

Showing inadequacy

Five-year-old Sean dilly-dallies over dressing himself and cannot 'work the buttons.' Morning after morning, his mother takes the bait, first nagging at him and then coming to his rescue. He is getting lots of attention by showing inadequacy, and he has come no nearer to learning to 'work the buttons.'

Discouraged children often show inadequacy. Their frustrated parents end up drawing attention to the inadequacy by criticising them or coming to their aid. The child may then feel more incapable and inadequate than ever. So there is no improvement.

The first step in dealing with 'inadequate' children is to stop rewarding the inadequacy by criticising it or drawing attention to it, and to look instead for an improvement – or even an *effort* at improvement – to encourage.

Approval of friends

Fifteen-year-old Trevor stays out late with his friends. In spite of his mother's scolding and lecturing, his time keeping shows no improvement.

As children get older, it becomes more and more important to them to impress their friends. This can lead to misbehaviour that worries or frightens parents. As a result, parents can easily fall into a pattern of disapproving and nagging.

If Trevor's mother scolds him in front of his friends, he will feel hurt and angry, and may become more hostile. She may do better to postpone dealing with the problem for the moment – if possible. Later, she will be able to deal with the issue more effectively – as we will see in the chapter on discipline.

out late with his friends

Summing up

These, then, are some of the main reasons why children misbehave – to get attention, power or revenge, to show inadequacy or to win the approval of their friends... They do not do these things consciously; they usually do not know *what* they are seeking when they misbehave. But giving in to them will only *reward* the misbehaviour and add to their misery instead of making them happy.

When there is misbehaviour, then, it helps to ask: "How am I feeling right now?" My feelings offer a clue to what my child is looking for. When I feel *annoyed*, the child is probably seeking *attention*; when I'm *angry*, the child's

LOOKING AFTER YOURSELF

You need space. Time for yourself. Every day. Too many parents are over-stretched, lose their sense of humour and warmth and fall back on tranquillisers because they have not taken time for self-care. **Your children need you to look after yourself!** They suffer when you neglect your own needs and become their doormat. When you are relaxed, you can love more naturally.

Self-care does not mean escaping to alcohol or television – it is about doing things that have nothing to do with your work or parenting – reading *your* kind of novel or magazine, playing your kind of music, having a massage, walking, meditating/praying, gardening, enjoying sport, doing yoga... It includes having your own friends and interests that help you feel relaxed and healthy. It may include lowering too-high parenting standards – and standard of tidiness! – so that you can put your own needs higher up the list of 'to-dos.' And it may include learning methods of relaxing and de-stressing – like pulling out of an angry exchange with a child and going off to do some vigorous exercise or talk with a friend until you have calmed down.

You might consider a weekly 'date with yourself' when you spend at least an hour – or a full morning – doing something creative or different. (This Weekly Date is explained well in Helen Cameron's book, *The Artist's Way*.) All this may sound selfish, but your children will benefit more from it than if you were totally focused on them!

11

goal is probably *power*; when I feel *hurt*, that tells me that the child is probably seeking *revenge*; a *helpless* feeling is usually a sign that the child is showing *inadequacy*; and when I feel *worried* or *alarmed*, my child may be seeking the *approval of friends*.

Once the child's goal is clear, **you can avoid taking the bait by not reacting in the usual way – you might even do the opposite to what you normally do.** If you normally shout, try lowering your voice. If you're normally quiet, try asserting yourself. Refuse to give attention on demand. Ignore tantrums or squabbling unless there is real danger. Back off when you find yourself becoming hooked into an argument. Look for something to encourage when you feel like criticising. In this way you can begin to change unthinking patterns of parenting that are not effective and you will no longer be rewarding misbehaviour.

Time together

There is probably no better way to 'act differently' than to be more affectionate. In this course, there is a lot of emphasis on parenting skills, but parenting is not *just* a matter of skills – the main challenge and task is to *love* our children. That means slowing down and taking time with them. Time to listen to their stories, to touch them and show them affection, to play and laugh and have fun together, to relax over food, to know the details of their lives and remember to ask about those details. Not "How are things?" but "How did your match go?" "Was Cindy there?" "How's her mother?" "Where did you go afterwards?" Telling children you love them will not work unless you *also* make the time to connect with them.

Giving this positive attention to children when they are not expecting it may be one of the best ways of doing the opposite to what we normally do and dealing more effectively with the *real* problems underlying their attention-seeking and power struggles.

My daughter looked at me in amazement and said "Mummy, what's wrong? You don't shout at me any more."

GETTING IN TOUCH

Tick any of the following things that upset you in any of your children. Would you like to add anything else to the list?

Won't get up in the mornings. Doesn't dress/ wash properly. Won't wash without being reminded. Leaves door open. Messes food. Has bad table manners. Answers back. Constantly fighting and squabbling. Throws tantrums. Moans, complains a lot. Is very slow. Rushes meals. Neglects or rushes homework. Uncooperative at home. Watches too much TV. Bullies. Tells lies. Doesn't communicate. Won't go to bed on time. Answers back. Shows lack of respect for others. Neglects pet dog or cat. Doesn't mix – no friends. Comes late for meals. Moody and depressed. Stays out too late. Something else...?

B. What do you normally do when this behaviour upsets you? – smack, scold, ignore the misbehaviour, remove the child, deprive the child of a treat, threaten, plead, promise rewards... What would you like to do instead?

PLANS FOR NEXT WEEK

1. Think of one example of ongoing misbehaviour where you are not being effective. Plan to do the unexpected, perhaps the opposite to what you usually do. There is no guarantee that this will work, but you have little to lose if you are not being effective at present! The more specific your plan is the better. It may help to write down what exactly you plan to do, who with, when, where, etc.

2. Consider asking yourself each evening next week (and perhaps each evening for the next 10 years!), "What one thing will I do tomorrow to give positive attention and affection to at least one of my children when it is not expected?"

3. Re-read the section, *Looking After Yourself*, and plan one thing you will do to care for *yourself* this week. (Caring for yourself may be one of the most important changes you need to make as a parent!)

Plans..._____

_____

Please read chapter 2 before the next meeting (and chapter 1 if you have not read it.)

TABLE 1: AVOIDING THE BAIT

The table below* sums up some of the main points in Chapter 1. Does it help you to see ways in which you could be more effective?

BAIT	PARENT SEES BAIT	AND GETS HOOKED IN	AVOIDING THE BAIT
Constant squabbling and fighting between Sarah and John. Loud screams and regular complaints to get mother's attention.	When a child seeks ATTENTION parent usually feels ANNOYED.	Mother rewards this behaviour by paying attention to it – trying to sort out fights, correcting, reminding, scolding... But misbehaviour soon continues. Her method is not effective.	Try to avoid getting involved in children's squabbles unless there is real danger. Refuse to give attention on demand. But make time for positive attention later when it is not expected.
11-year-old Mike refuses point-blank to clear his dishes off the table or help with the washing-up.	When child enters POWER contest, parent may feel ANGRY.	Mike's father argues, scolds, then forces his son to obey. Mike hates father and secretly plots revenge.	It is usually more effective not to seek to win power struggles. Pull out of the fight, but do arrange to talk it out later, when everyone is calmer.
15-year-old Marie has refused to speak to her father for three weeks.	When child seeks REVENGE parent may feel VERY HURT.	Father rants and raves about what will happen if she continues to refuse to speak to him. She only becomes more entrenched and bitter.	It is unhelpful to play the retaliation game with your children. When you stay friendly and cheerful, the atmosphere will gradually improve.
8-year-old George is slow and awkward – and has no friends.	When a child shows INADEQUACY, parent may feel HOPELESS or HELPLESS.	George's parents sometimes coax, sometimes nag, sometimes give up on him. They often take pity on him and take over his tasks. George shows no improvement.	Neither criticism nor taking over tasks is helpful. Keep on the lookout for efforts or improvements and encourage by 'noticing' them quietly.
13-year-old Evelyn has lost interest in studying and has begun to stay out later and later in the evenings.	When a child seeks the APPROVAL of FRIENDS parents may feel WORRIED/ ANXIOUS.	Evelyn's parents scold, nag and threaten. There are constant rows and bad feelings. The atmosphere in the house is depressing and unpleasant.	Try showing interest in Evelyn and her friends, and make time for chats with her. For more serious problems, however, action may be more effective than talking – see chapter 6.

*This Table is based on the discoveries and thinking of Alfred Adler as developed by Rudolf Dreikurs, Don Dinkmeyer and Gary McKay.

CASE STUDIES

Read the following conversations (it's more fun if two or three people read them aloud). Then, in groups of three, discuss the questions at the end of each situation.

MOTHER: *(annoyed)* Jim, what have I said to you about dumping your schoolbag in the front room! And look where you've thrown your jacket!
JIM: *(resentful)* I'll pick them up in a minute.
Half an hour later...
MOTHER: *(angrily)* Hey, I thought you were going to take these things out of the room!
JIM: Ah, get off my back. I told you I was going to do it. Give me a chance, will you!
MOTHER: *(angrily)* Look, if you don't pick up your bag and your jacket and get them out of here quickly, I'll... I'll... You'll see what'll happen to you! Now I'm warning you!
Eventually, after more nagging and threatening, Jim removed his belongings – though he proceeded to dump his schoolbag in the passageway outside his bedroom.

By the end of this situation, the mother is angry. In Table 1 anger is the clue that she may be getting locked into a power struggle. Can you see ways in which she is being ineffective, perhaps even rewarding Jim's behaviour?

FATHER: What are you two doing out of bed? Get back up those stairs!
JANE: But Dad, Sonya pulled my hair.
FATHER: Sonya! Did you? Did you pull her hair?
SONYA: I didn't mean to pull it.
JANE: Yes, you did!
SONYA: No, I didn't... Anyway, you were singing and you wouldn't let me get to sleep!
FATHER: *(annoyed)* I don't know which of you is the worst! But Sonya, you're older and you ought to know better! Now, up the stairs this instant, and if there's another sound from either of you, I'll go up and smack you!

Father is annoyed in this situation – a clue that his children may be seeking attention. How is he being ineffective – and actually rewarding the squabbling?

GARY: *(giggling with his friend, Clive)* Huh, I've spilt my milk. *(More giggles).*
MOTHER: *(annoyed)* Now look what you've done! What's come over you this evening, Gary? You usually behave yourself at the table!
GARY: *(desperate to impress Clive)* No I don't! These stupid glasses are too easy to knock over anyway.
MOTHER: *(angry)* Gary, don't talk to me like that. I won't have it.
GARY: *(mimicking)* I won't have it! I won't have it! (More giggles).
MOTHER: *(angrily)* Go to your bedroom this instant!
GARY: Good. I don't want your stinking food. Coming, Clive?

Why might Gary be acting like this? How is his mother being ineffective?

CHAPTER 2: BECOMING A RESPONSIBLE PARENT

Five-year-old Tom cannot dress himself. Every morning his mother keeps telling him to start dressing, then makes empty threats about what will happen if he does not make an effort – and then scolds him crossly as she dresses him herself. Tom has learnt how good it is to be helpless – he gets attention from his mother and gets dressed into the bargain. She does not realise that instead of training Tom to dress himself, she is actually training him *not* to be responsible for himself.

Twelve-year-old Jane is not expected to do any chores at home. Her mother cooks, clears up after meals, washes her clothes, irons them, makes Jane's bed and tidies her room. "I don't mind," her mother says, "I love her and I don't want to spoil her childhood. I don't want her to go through what I went through when I was a little girl." Jane's mother would be shocked if someone pointed out to her that she is helping Jane to become lazy and irresponsible.

The first generation in history…
In both of the examples above, the parents mean well but are ineffective.

They may be spending themselves for their children, doing what they think good parents ought to do. But they do not seem to be asking the important question, "What will help my children to become more mature and responsible?"

In the past, children were treated abusively and had to work long hours, even in shocking conditions down mines. Nobody would want to go back to that, but suddenly the opposite is true – almost nothing is expected of children. Ours is the first generation in history in which they are not expected to work at home. We are often happy if they are not bothering us – though they may be idle for hours on end, playing computer games, watching TV or moping in a bedroom. **Children who are stretched, stimulated and given responsibility can develop a far greater sense of responsibility for themselves.** We need to expect a lot more of them if we want to ease them into adulthood without an overlong and unnecessarily painful adolescence. At the very least they need to take responsibility for clearing up after themselves.

Should we pay children?

Would it help to pay children for the work they do at home? It is hardly a good idea to pay for basic household tasks like making their own beds or clearing up after meals. That is part of belonging to a family. But you may like to consider paying for heavier work like washing windows, weeding, etc.

As to pocket money itself, it *may* help to foster responsibility if you give your children a weekly money allowance instead of constantly handing out money for school-snacks, treats, discos, etc. That can help to make them responsible for balancing their own budgets. We know of a number of teenagers who wanted only label clothes until they were given a monthly clothing allowance!

I was a slave all these years, lifting and laying them, waiting on them hand and foot. Without realising it, I was training them to grow up expecting others to serve them. What kind of marriages would they make with that attitude!

Changing ourselves.

In developing a sense of responsibility in children, we might begin by looking at ourselves. Take sex roles, for example. Children learn a great deal about the roles of men and women from the way we behave – and from what we expect of them. Think how different a boy's training for life is when he is expected to cook, clean, sew, etc., and when he sees an adult man doing household chores. And why shouldn't our daughters learn to change a wheel, use a screwdriver,

change an electric plug and dig the garden? **Even children in the first few years of primary school, boys as well as girls, can perform many household tasks when they are *expected* to do them!** They may resent your attempts to stretch them at first, but they soon become engrossed in something new.

Parents of teenagers sometimes think: "It's too late now for me to change!" But it is never too late to change. That is probably the most important truth in Virginia Satir's book, 'Peoplemaking.' No matter how bad the situation in your family is, no matter how hopeless it may appear, there is always hope. **Change is always possible – in every important aspect of family life.** That is not theory; it comes out of a great deal of experience.

Being a 'good' parent.

One of the major changes that this course encourages is to stop being a 'good' parent and become instead a responsible one.

'Good' parents often act like servants, doing far too much for their children. They remind them, coax them, pick up their clothes, make their school lunches, help with dressing them, supervise their eating, settle their fights, etc., etc.

In spite of all our good intentions, we may be harming our children if we are merely 'good' parents. If we take on our children's responsibilities, we run the risk of making them over-dependent (or rebellious). And if they are not allowed to learn form experience or from the consequences of their actions, they may grow up lacking in confidence because so many of their choices will have been made for them.

Being a responsible parent.

An alternative to being a 'good' parent is to be a *responsible* one. Responsible parents respect their children, encouraging them as far as possible to make their own decisions and to live with the consequences of those

picking up their clothes, making their lunches, settling their fights...

decisions. Very often, 'good' parents do not show this respect to their children. And they do not respect *themselves* when they allow their children to treat them as servants.

Children can become remarkably responsible when they are given responsibility. Seven-year-olds can make their own school lunches; children of all ages can settle their own fights; they can have their own alarm-clocks and take responsibility for getting themselves up in the morning – or face the consequences of being late for school. All this saves a lot of wear and tear on parents. And it is a more effective and responsible approach.

Responsible parents are firm but not controlling. They respect their children's rights and expect to be given their own rights. If your youngsters are playing too noisily in the kitchen, you might say, "The noise is too much for me. Do something quietly in the kitchen or make as much noise as you like outside. Which do you want to do?" With this calm approach, you claim your own rights and respect them in making their own choices. That is much more effective than nagging, forbidding or taking away a child's freedom to choose.

Or take the case of your son who is always 'losing' things. As long as he has

'good' parents who keep finding his missing shoes, toys, etc., for him, he may not learn to care about his belongings. **When you stop rescuing him and allow him to live with the *consequences* of his carelessness, he can quickly become more responsible.** Respecting him like this will also help him grow in maturity and build his self-confidence.

Developing responsibility, then, does not just mean handing over more *tasks* to your children. It also includes giving them increasing freedom to make their *own* decisions and to choose what they will wear and eat and buy.

The need for training and guidance. This is not to suggest that everything children do is now a matter of choice for them. 'Latchkey kids' are given too much freedom and choice – without supervision, support or a guiding hand. There will be some things that are not choices: it is natural to expect co-operation in the running of a household, respect for others – and courtesies like 'please,' 'thank you' and saying hello to visitors.

When we do allow children more choice and freedom, that has to be given gradually, in stages, and with time set aside for *training*, at times challenging their behaviour and offering guidance. For example, it may not be enough just to say "Settle your own squabbles." You may need to sit down with a child from time to time to talk out ways of dealing non-violently with conflict. Sadly, some parents are reluctant to offer guidance or make demands on their children, fearful that this might harm them. But **guidance is what parents are for!** The only concern is that we offer it in ways that will be effective.

How to provide training
In training children, it helps to start with easy tasks and to increase them gradually. You may find the following four steps helpful in doing this:

1. Tell them what to do.

2. Show them.

3. Let them try it with supervision.

4. Back off gradually, but continue to notice and encourage their contributions occasionally – in a low-key way, not going overboard with praise!

The best time to train a young person is when you have set time aside, you feel unhurried, and you are relaxed about how the task will turn out. Remember that **building a bond with your son or daughter is much more important than how well they perform the task**. You are there as a kind of friendly presence, encouraging, asking questions, showing, letting them try things for themselves, pleased to see them making an effort, improving, growing. You are close by as they fumble, concentrate, try again, improve... You are there as they learn to dress, wash their teeth, tie their shoes, cross the road, ride a bike, wash their own hair, cook a meal, play the guitar, tackle new school work, wash and dry dishes, vacuum... With a parent beside them a new challenge can be fun.

This can be time-consuming to begin with. A simple job that you might have done in seconds will take longer to do and will not be as well done! You will need to lower your high standards and have lots of patience!

In the long term, however, you have a great deal to gain. Your eighteen-year-olds will be cooking a meal at least once a week, buying, washing and ironing their own clothes, cleaning, vacuuming, ready to leave home. You will have less to do when the household tasks are shared, and your children will be better prepared for the real world, more responsible, more co-operative and more caring.

I have involved my son in clearing up after meals and we've had our best chats together as he washes and I dry. There is something about working together without facing each other that makes it easier to talk about things.

YOUR CHILDREN AND THE POP-CULTURE

Concerns about pop-culture/ media

There is concern among parent educators about the amount of exposure children have to the pop-culture – in magazines, music, advertising, television and computer games. Many children spend more time in front of a television or games machine than they spend at school, and the sheer inactivity of sitting in front of a screen for so long is depriving them of the fun of running, playing, cycling, reading, talking…

There is even more serious concern about the values being fed to children through this enormously seductive pop-culture. These values include violence and shouting to get your own way, acting on your feelings, the tyranny of 'cool,' and the demand for instant satisfaction of your wants – all reinforced by computer games where you can set your own levels of frustration instead of learning to deal with anger in the normal ways.

In the absence of adults from many young people's lives, these pressures are powerfully reinforced by children's 'second family' – the peer group of boys and girls at school and in the neighbourhood. Children have never been so connected to other children as they are today, and they have never been less connected to adults. Instead of gradually discovering their unique identity, they are getting their self-esteem from trying to fit in with friends who are themselves driven by the pop-

culture and are even vying with one another in being cooler than each other. This 'second family' now takes over from parents in terms of influence from as young as age seven. And all this affects a parent's most fundamental task – the protection and nurturing of the child's core identity and self-esteem. What can be done?

How to protect and nurture in these circumstances

Leading educators like Taffel and Biddulph suggest we encourage TV programmes that are wholesome or educational, but that we negotiate with our children to limit access to TV, Internet and computer games as much as possible. We might also insist that they plan in advance what they are going to watch. If this sounds drastic, maybe it needs to be seen in the context of what we put in *place* of these media. How will children spend their time?

First, we need to encourage *interests* – a musical instrument, sport (any game but computer games!) cooking, art, cycling or anything that *attracts* your child. (Children also build healthier *friendships* around hobbies or activities.) Interests might include a daily dose of exercising their bodies to work off the cooped-up restlessness that builds up from sitting around watching tense TV and computer game situations. Play might also include the rough and tumble play and wrestling that dads tend to be so good at.

Secondly, as we see from this chapter, we need to expect children to *work* at home as well as to play.

Finally, and most important, we need to provide an *alternative* to the values of the pop-culture by connecting and spending time with our children (including some time watching TV with them and talking about it). For the same reasons we need to find ways to expose children more to the conversation and influence of adults whom we trust.

GETTING
IN
TOUCH

Here are some things parents do for their children – which their children (depending on their ages) might do for themselves. Study the list and tick off anything you do which you think your children might be capable of doing. Then ask yourself at what age children might be capable of each of these responsibilities.

**Get them up in the mornings;
Dress their beds; tidy their rooms;
Choose and lay out their clothes for the following day;
Dress them; tie their shoes;
Dress or change the baby;
Choose and buy their clothes;
Make school lunches; prepare breakfast; cook; prepare their meals;
Pick up their clothes; tidy away their toys;
Bath them; wash faces; brush teeth; wash their hair; comb hair;
Supervise their eating;
Iron their clothes; sew; knit;
Sweep the kitchen floor; dust the house; vacuum the floor;**

**Lay the table and clear it;
Clean and tidy the bathroom; clean windows;
Sort out and fold newly washed clothes;
Settle fights and squabbles;
Go to the post office/ shop;
Do all their homework with them;
Clean the car; change the oil;
Paint inside and outside the house;
Mow the lawn; plant flowers and vegetables; weed;
Mend bicycle punctures;
Wire an electric plug; change a fuse;
Use saw/hammer; chop firewood;
Make the decisions about their routines, their friends, their lifestyle, their future.**

PLANS
FOR NEXT
WEEK

1. What are you doing that your children could do for themselves? Choose one new responsibility (perhaps from the list above) that you will introduce during the next week. Be as specific as possible: How will you start? Who with? When? You may like to write your plans...
2. In doing this course, try to get the backing of any other adults who live with you (a partner, your mother…) you might plan to involve them by loaning them the book or video and talking the ideas through with them.

Plans..._____

Please read chapter three of this handbook before the next session

TABLE 2 – WHICH KIND OF PARENT?

Parents are asked to consider the two types of parent in the table below. Do you think the parents' behaviour has the effect shown in the second and fourth columns?

'GOOD' PARENT TYPES		PARENTS WHO DEVELOP RESPONSIBILITY	
Behaviour	**Effect**	**Behaviour**	**Effect**
1. Controls by punishment or by rewards. Is always right. Expects obedience and has to win.	Child may fight back or give up. Becomes dishonest, tells lies. Doesn't learn self-control.	Parent allows child to make decisions. Positive and encouraging.	Child tends to grow in confidence. Learns decision-making.
2. Wants perfection. Finds fault constantly. Needs child to behave so neighbours will approve.	Child may become discouraged – can't measure up. May try to be 'perfect.' Over-anxious about pleasing.	Parent does not expect adult standards, is happy with improvements and encourages child's strengths.	Child usually gains belief in self and becomes more willing to 'have a go.'
3. Suspicious. Doesn't trust child. Hedges child in with rules and regulations.	Child may feel guilty and tend to distrust others.	Parent trusts child and looks for efforts to encourage.	Child grows in freedom and belief in self. Learns to trust others.
4. Feels superior and takes over child's responsibilities. Over-protective, pities, shames.	Child feels helpless. Expects others to do everything.	Parent shows respect for child and encourages responsibility.	Child will tend to learn self-respect and become more responsible.
5. Cannot say no. Constantly gives in to child. Becomes doormat.	Child may become 'spoilt' and selfish and find it more difficult to make friends.	Parent is firm. Respects own rights and child's rights. Encourages co-operation.	Child more likely to learn to co-operate – and to make friends more easily.

CASE STUDIES

Read the following conversations (it may be better if two or three people read them aloud). Then, in groups of three, discuss the questions at the end of each conversation.

JILL (13): Dad, will you drive me down to the swimming pool? I need to be there for seven.
FATHER: Look, Jill, this is becoming a habit! I'm in the middle of something now and I can't leave it. Why didn't you think of going earlier and you could have taken your bike?
JILL: Well, I just forgot, and I'm going to be late if you don't take me (almost in tears). Please, Dad, will you?
FATHER: *(with a sigh)* All right, I'll do it this time, but you really ought to think ahead.

Parents need to be available for genuine emergencies – but not for regularly occurring 'emergencies' that could have been foreseen and that are the result of carelessness or forgetfulness. In what ways was this father a 'good' parent rather than a responsible one? What could he have done instead to encourage responsibility in Jill?

FATHER: Patricia! What are you at? You're slobbering your food there like a little pig. *(pause)* Patricia! Did you hear what I said to you? It's disgusting to sit here and watch you! Use your spoon... No, not that hand, the other hand... Hold it steady. Steady! Aaah! Now look what you've done, stupid! Quick! Someone get a cloth and wipe it up!

In what ways is the father helping Patricia not to be responsible? What might he have done instead to help her learn better table manners?

MOTHER *(speaking to nine year old son)*: Come on, John, it's your bedtime. Quickly! Look at the time. You know I shouldn't have to remind you night after night!
(Two minutes later...) John! I said it's bedtime. Now that's it! Come on, your supper's on the table five minutes... That's it, now, drink it up... Now your teeth... Where's your toothbrush?... Ah, come on now, this is crazy. You know where you're supposed to keep your toothbrush... Here it is. Now, don't be a minute – I'll get your pyjamas... Have you been to the toilet?...

In what ways is the mother a 'good' parent rather than a responsible one? What could she have done instead to encourage responsibility in John?

CHAPTER 3: ENCOURAGING CHILDREN

Jane (12) and Teresa (14) have just received their school reports. Jane comes rushing to her mother to show her how well she has done.

Mother: This is wonderful, dear. And look at your maths. Ninety-two! It's fantastic. Wait 'till your father sees this. He'll be so proud! But what about Teresa – where is she?

Jane: Oh, you know her. She just threw her report on the floor.

Mother: What? Teresa! Come here this minute. And bring me your report, miss!

Teresa: *(Handing over report)* You won't like it.

Mother: Uh! I certainly don't… My God, look at your geography, this is a disgrace. You've made no effort. Why can't you work like Jane instead of letting us all down like this! Honestly. I don't know what's going to become of you!

In this incident, Teresa is already a discouraged child. Her mother is adding to her discouragement – expecting little of her, criticising her and comparing her to her younger sister.

What is less obvious is that this mother may also be discouraging *Jane*. For, as we will see, **a certain kind of praise often discourages children from making their own decisions and makes them over-dependant on what their parents think of them**.

How parents discourage children

In many homes, we try to improve our children by concentrating on their mistakes. We criticise, nag, threaten, scold, shame or boss them. We don't do this deliberately – and we wouldn't dream of doing it if we had any idea of how damaging it can be. For children come to believe these negative messages from their parents. As a result, they can carry around guilt, discouragement and dislike of themselves, even for the rest of their lives.

There are other ways in which we discourage children without being aware of what we are doing. We discourage when we make too many decisions for them (which gives the message that they are not capable of making the decisions

24

themselves). We discourage when our standards are too high. And when we compare one child to another, which often discourages the weaker child. We mean well, but the effect is often the opposite to what we would have wanted.

Don't we need to correct!

But doesn't children's behaviour need to be corrected? How can we be expected to encourage a child who is misbehaving and cannot be ignored?

It is true that we need to correct and guide, but it is important to separate the deed from the doer so that we correct the deed without attacking the child. For example, Bart can be told it is wrong to hit the baby, but not that *he* is naughty or bad. Marion can be asked to wipe up the milk she has spilt, but there is no need to raise your voice or shout at her – a correction given in a calm voice is more effective. As it progresses, this course aims to give parents skills in correcting misbehaviour more effectively.

My God, look at your geography!

Moreover, psychologists tell us that **misbehaviour gets worse when we notice it and draw attention to it.** For example, children's squabbles and fights may be best ignored as long as they are not dangerous – we have seen that children often squabble merely to *gain* our attention. Similarly, it may be best not to listen to children telling tales on each other. Life becomes simpler when

they get the message that we are not interested in finding culprits or listening to tattling. On the other hand, **good behaviour also increases when we draw attention to it. When we notice and comment on positive behaviour, we reinforce it!**

Noticing positive behaviour

When we are on the lookout for small efforts and improvements instead of mistakes, children grow in confidence and make great strides. 'You got ten out of twenty right' is so much more helpful a comment than: 'You got ten out of twenty wrong.' It helps to look on the positive side, to be happy with *effort* – one step at a time – rather than to look for success or final results. Brenda may not be great at washing dishes, but she may be good at clearing the table after meals, so it will help to notice her contribution there.

And we have seen how much it encourages young people to give them responsibility. It tells them: "I trust you. You are a responsible person."

When I asked Maurice to cut the grass, he said: "You expect me to be your slave and do everything around here!" I said: "Maurice, I'd be glad if you would do it, but you don't have to. In fact, two weeks ago the grass was quite long and I was surprised that you made such a clean job of it. So you've already done more than your fair share." Then I left him. A few minutes later he was out working like a Trojan at the grass. The few words of encouragement had made the difference.

What encourages children?

Encouraging is not just a skill, however. Skills may help, but they can never make up for a lack of love. **Children need to know that they are special to you and that you will always love them, even when they misbehave.**

Psychologist Steve Biddulph claims that children need two kinds of love –

firmlove and *softlove* (what we prefer to call *gentlelove)*. Both are vital. We will deal with firmlove in another section of this book, but gentlelove is the foundation without which firmlove will crumble. It is like sunshine for a plant, providing the affection and touch and warmth that allow children to feel welcome and good about themselves and to grow in love and confidence.

You will not always *feel* this affection, but the more you can put the pressures of modern life to one side and relax with your children, the more your loving feelings and enjoyment of them can surface. For that is the key to gentlelove – being relaxed and available to waste time with your children – even if it means both parents choosing less demanding careers and having less money! Loving words do not count if you are not around for playing games, telling stories, hugging, play-wrestling, praying with them (if prayer is a part of your life), taking them cycling and shopping and on trips, chatting about the details of their lives and having fun with them. All this is time-consuming, but it builds great memories of being loved. When children know that they are special to you, that you enjoy their company and they don't have to earn your love, they learn that they are loveable and good – and you'll have given them great security for life.

Thanks for taking the baby – it gave me a break.

The difference between praise and encouragement

In building up children's confidence, it helps to be aware of the difference between praise and encouragement. Some years ago, a psychotherapist and author, Dr Haim Ginnott, made us aware of this difference. Praise, he pointed out, tends to concentrate on success. It notices the winner who comes first but ignores the *efforts* and the *improvements* made by those who *failed* to come first. Praise also gives *my* judgement of my children's behaviour instead of helping children to form their own judgement. And it may sound insincere and gushy, often leaving a child uncomfortable and over-anxious about the good opinion of others instead of encouraging self-reliance and confidence.

Can you see how the following are examples of praise? "You're great!" "You're a very good girl!" "You've won – that's terrific!" In these cases, parents are giving their *own* judgements, not helping children to judge for themselves. Sometimes, of course, these comments may be okay, as when a child has gained some genuine success or achievement. But even then we are best not to overdo praise or exaggerate or compare. **The real test is: am I encouraging my child to be more confident and self-assured, to have more belief in herself, to be more at ease with himself?' Praise may not have that effect.**

Effective ways of encouraging

We all want the best for our children. We want them to live without the nagging and the put-downs that were part of childhood for so many of us. So we'll round off this chapter by mentioning some ways of encouraging without praising or going to extremes:

1. Instead of giving your judgement of a child, "You're a terrific worker" or "You're much better than Karen," you might **point out the good *effects* of what your child did** "That makes my work easier" "Thanks for taking the baby – it gave me a break." Children can

see these effects for themselves, but they may be embarrassed or unable to cope with a judgement like "You're wonderful!" that they feel they cannot live up to. Note that speaking *personally* (using I or me) also made the statements above more believable.

2. ***Show confidence* in children's ability without exaggerating or being gushy.** "I was surprised the last time you cut the grass – it was quite long. I know you'll be able to manage now." But not: "You're brilliant!" or "Your drawing is excellent." Help them to become less dependent on what *you* think by asking, "What do you think yourself?" Or show confidence with a nod of the head or a simple comment like, "Sounds good"/ "Okay"/ "Good point."

3. **Notice *improvement* and *effort*.** "That's great – the room looks a lot tidier." "Well done – a month ago you could only swim two lengths." "You've spent a full hour working at that – I'm impressed." "I notice you're getting along much better with Bill recently." The world we live in rewards *success*, so children can become discouraged without your support and encouragement for their *efforts*. But don't spoil it all by adding a comment about how much more they are capable of doing!

4. Since one of our goals is to encourage co-operation, you might **keep an eye open for small contributions** – anything helpful or thoughtful or considerate. Don't go to town with, "You're so helpful and thoughtful!" – just notice the contribution with a simple, "Thanks for your help," or, "I appreciate what you did for Jane." Even saying, "I need your help with..." – can be encouraging to a child.

5. **Speak *calmly* and *positively*, even when giving a correction.** "Stay on the footpath" is more effective than planting ideas like, "Don't walk on the road!"

6. The sixth and most important way of encouraging children is to **make the time to give them buckets of gentlelove**. It often helps to *plan* this time with them, but you need to bear in mind that being an affectionate parent is much more about being available at the many *unplanned* times when they need you or when *they* are ready for fun!

Every morning, on the way to work, I think of at least one thing I'll do with my daughter or son that evening. A game of cards, a story, a wrestle on the floor – something I wouldn't normally do when I'm just drifting. Yesterday, I had to unblock the sink and I decided to let Nick do it with me. We were a lot slower, but he learned things and he was proud of himself by the end of it.

THE PLACE OF FATHERS

An involved father

Many of us grew up with a distant father whose duties often stopped at earning money for the family – and gruffly enforcing discipline. Sadly, many fathers are still absent from their children's lives, perhaps separated from the mother and no longer in contact – or working long hours and coming home exhausted. The absence of an involved father has now been linked to problems in children's behaviour and the abuse of drugs – but we also know that an involved father can have a powerful influence for good on his children, especially on boys. Most men care deeply about their children and *want* to be more involved with them: it is the structures of work and society that are the real culprits.

In recent years, more fathers are becoming involved with their families, but most men still do not know the 'boring' details of their children's lives – like the size of their shoes or the names of their best friends. When both partners are asked to make lists of who does what, even the 25% of fathers who describe themselves as 'very involved' are shocked at how long the mother's list is. Yet Dr Ron Taffel has shown how children tend to bond with and confide in the parent who deals with the details of their daily lives.

Male strengths are different

One obvious solution is to share out the endless list of tasks so that the father gets engaged, not just in playing football but in the daily grind of thankless tasks – bedtime, bathtime, tidy-up time, etc. A woman needs to go gently, however, and to be realistic, to aim for a small change at a time, not for an ideal – it never helps to change someone by telling him how useless he is. She also needs to be careful to allow for a man's different standards: fathers are not mothers, and when he is left in charge, it is possible that the children will go to bed late and eat nothing but hamburgers, but they may have had the *fun* they needed!

This is one of the strengths of men – they are often good at providing the fun and antics that young people of all ages appreciate – and the play-wrestling and touch that their sons love. And these activities can also offer opportunities for modelling fair play, good humour, allowing the child to win much of the time and so on. A man also has an important influence when he *does* things along with his children (things like gardening, fixing a car, washing dishes, working in the shed, clearing the yard…). It is good for a father to be on the lookout for opportunities to involve his children in doing things along with him. But he needs to be *relaxed* about these activities and realise that *connecting* with and *enjoying* his children is more important than getting the job done! Letting his children handle a screwdriver, a brush or a saw will slow him down – but letting go like that usually helps him to enjoy his son or daughter more!

Not fitting into sexist roles

Too often in the past a mother allowed herself to be a doormat and a 'soft touch' for her children while the father was the iron fist in the background when things got out of hand. It is *important* to be able to provide backup and support for each other, but such a partnership was hardly a good model for young people, nor is it fair to either parent – both need to develop a gentle and a firm side. When there is an angry scene, for example, between a mother and her child, a father is better not to wade in to settle the row but to step in to offer backup. He might insist that the child settle the row without shouting at or disrespecting the mother, then he can withdraw to a safe distance and let them settle it themselves.

GETTING IN TOUCH

How often do you *make these (or similar) remarks? Put a tick for each statement in the appropriate column.*

	Never	Sometimes	Often
DISCOURAGING			
Nag, nag, nag ...			
Don't... Don't... Don't			
Not now, I'm busy!			
Why can't you be like ...			
You're a cheeky...			
PRAISING			
What a beautiful picture!			
You're terrific!			
You look so wonderful!			
You're such a good boy!			
ENCOURAGING			
Thank you. That helps me.			
So that's how you do it!			
Well done. You've improved.			
Will you help me with...?			

PLANS FOR NEXT WEEK

1. Who is your most discouraged child? In what ways can you encourage that child during the next week? Possibilities include: Being on the lookout for efforts and improvements and 'noticing' them; trusting with more responsibilities; saying thanks, please, sorry and generally showing respect; spending more time with him, having fun with her, catching up, listening...

Plans... _____

You may like to write below what you plan to do.

2. It is harder to be positive with children when you are too stressed. Experiment with some of the following suggestions over the next few weeks to find out what helps *you* to de-stress when you are feeling angry or tense:
a.) Say calming things to yourself like, "Relax... I can handle this."
b.) Leave the room or count to ten.
c.) Go for a brisk walk in the fresh air.
d.) Sit or lie and breathe more deeply.
e.) Talk to someone, even on the phone
f.) Ring a Parent line.

Please read chapter four of this handbook before the next session

TABLE 3: ENCOURAGEMENT

Below are eight types of parent that often discourage, and eight corresponding types that usually encourage. Can you see yourself in some of them? What have you found helps to make children happier and build their confidence and belief in themselves?

DISCOURAGING PARENT	TYPICAL REMARKS	ENCOURAGING PARENT	TYPICAL REMARKS
1. Looks for success rather than effort.	'You got five wrong out of ten. You'll have to do better than that!'	Looks for little efforts rather than success. Relaxed and accepting.'	'You got five right out of ten. Well done. You seem to be making a greater effort recently.'
2. Wants achievements rather than improvements. Compares child to others.	'Look at Andrew how well he can do it! You're just wasting my time as well as your own!'	Happy with small *improvements* rather than big achievements.	'That's it. Now you're getting the hang of it!'
3. Does too much for children; becomes their servant.	'I'll find your shoe when I've combed your hair – just be patient.'	Develops responsibility. Allows child to experiment and make mistakes.	'Now, add in the eggs and see what happens...'
4. Takes bait and reacts to child; authoritarian.	'Shut up and get out – and don't you dare talk to me like that again!'	Listens and shows interest in child.	'I see. So it's been very hard for you this week...'
5. Praises. Often insincere. Doesn't speak *personally*.	'You're absolutely gorgeous. Everyone will love you!'	Makes personal statements; sincere.	'I like your dress – it matches your hair and brings out the colour of your eyes.
6. Consoles, reassures, advises.	'Of course you did the right thing, dear – you always do.'	Listens. Allows child to judge for self.	'So what do you think yourself? How do you feel now about what you did?'
7. Threatens, gives orders, scolds, controls, reminds.	'Come on! Get up to your bed this instant or I'll...' *(for fifth time)*	Encourages child to make own decisions and live with the consequences.	'Oh well. We all make mistakes ... What can you learn from it all?'
8. Criticises; looks out for and points out mistakes.	'Now look what you've done! That was so stupid?'	Looks out for positive; is generally good-humoured.	'Oops! Now look what we've done! I'm glad you're with me, or I'd be stuck!'

CASE STUDIES

Read the following conversations (or a few people might read them aloud). Then, in groups of three discuss the questions that follow.

Gwen (15) is anxious, afraid she'll fail her exam next week.

What unhelpful things do parents often do or say in a situation like this? What could her parents do or say, or what questions might they ask – avoiding criticism and avoiding exaggerated praise – to help Gwen grow in confidence and belief in herself?

Michael (5) has just made his own bed, but the bedclothes are quite twisted and uneven. When his mother comes in, Michael obviously expects praise as he says:
'Look, Mummy, I've made my bed all by myself.'

What insincere (or critical) things do parents sometimes say in a situation like this? How might his mother train Michael to make a bed and help him feel good about himself and his efforts?

JANE (10): "Will you help me with this homework, Dad? I just can't do it."

In a situation like this, what do some parents do or say that might not be helpful? How could you encourage Jane – not just taking over and doing everything for her?

CHAPTER 4: LISTENING

Mr Potter has just come home from work. He is in a grumpy, unpleasant mood and has already complained about the noise from the radio. One of the children turned down the volume, but he is not satisfied.

"If you don't turn off that radio this instant," he says, "I'll get up and break the bloody thing!"

Controlling our feelings.
This incident illustrates a common problem in families – blaming the children when we are annoyed or angry instead of taking responsibility for our own feelings. We fail to recognise that our feelings come from inside us and depend on what we believe. If I think children should do exactly what I say, for example, I may be *upset* when they act differently. If I think they should *choose* how to act, then I may be *proud* to see them make their own decisions. **We can learn, then, to change our feelings by changing the way we look at or *think* about a situation** – otherwise we may be burying our anger alive to simmer under the surface and

then explode. It is frightening for young people to be exposed to very strong adult feelings.

Another healthy way to control strong feelings is to pull back when there is conflict and take half an hour to calm down before dealing with the situation – you might calm yourself by doing vigorous exercise or talking your feelings out with a partner or friend.

Whatever you do, it is important not to judge your feelings: parents may feel murderous rage towards their children, but these feelings are not *wrong* – as long as they are not acted on. Similarly, we may feel discouraged and see ourselves as failures when our children cause problems, but all young people seem to have their own tasks in life – parents did not create these difficulties and should try to put feelings of guilt aside in dealing with them.

Non-listening – and its effects.
So much for parents' feelings. It is only in recent years that we have come to see how important *children's* feelings are – recognising what is going on inside them

and giving them a sense of being understood. **This understanding can free children from deep-seated feelings that are at the root of much of their misbehaviour.**

So let's think about how we normally deal with their feelings. What do we say when they tell us about some trouble they have got into? Or are they afraid to tell us because they know we are going to lecture or scold them? When we do offer advice, it is well intentioned but may be ill timed and not nearly as effective as listening. And too often our first response is to cross-question, preach, criticise – or even *console*!

For consoling, too, can sometimes be a form of non-listening. Some of us cannot bear to see our children in difficulties or unhappy, but life is not always happy: they have to face difficulties, not avoid them, if they are to grow. Our goal is to help them learn by facing up to and handling their own problems. When they meet problems and feel upset, then, it will not help to say, "Don't cry," or "Don't be angry," or, "You'll feel okay tomorrow" or, "Don't worry, I'll buy you another one." We mean well, but we are not giving our young people what they *most* need in these cases, a sense of being listened to and understood and a chance to express and clear their feelings.

Helping children with their feelings
Children who are distressed need to express their hurt. They often do this in screams, tears, shaking, laughing, or shouting – we now know, for example, that crying releases healing chemicals in the body. Children may need to be held firmly to prevent them from hurting others or doing damage, but **it is important that we *encourage* the release of feelings rather than attempt to distract the child or suggest that boys should not cry or girls should not be angry**. When they are upset, children need our full attention, touching or hugging them if necessary, so that they can express their upset feelings and be

free to move on. This is an important form of listening. A parent's attention and understanding communicate respect, acceptance and love. And this frees a child to change, to love and to grow as a person.

If you don't turn off that radio, I'll break the bloody thing!

How to listen effectively.
Listening like that does not come naturally, but it is a skill that improves with practice. Here are some ways to become a better listener:

Make yourself more available. If you are too absorbed in television or always busy, you will miss out on many opportunities to provide the 'gentlelove' and affection that we have seen is so vital for young people. **There are also special times when it helps to set everything aside and concentrate on listening: when they come home from school; at bedtime; and whenever they seem to have strong feelings (upset, excited, or depressed, for example).**

As soon as you start to listen, it is good to make a mental switch – there may be little point in listening to the details of a football match if you consider it 'boring' and can't wait to get back to what you were at. You can *decide* to be interested and to enjoy being with your child. This is the importance of listening not only with your ears but also with your whole body

LONE PARENTING

There are certain advantages to being a lone parent – compared, for example, to a couple who are openly critical of one another in front of their children. But it is not easy trying to cope with all the deadlines and pressures of modern living with just one pair of hands and without the social support of another adult. Here are some suggestions that may help:

1. Lessen the burden. As soon as practicable, involve your children in the household tasks – vacuuming, washing, cooking, cleaning… They need time to play and to study, but work is also *good* for them as well as for you, and time training them will pay off.

2. Find social support from family and/or friends. You need adult company and interests outside the home. It is also unfair to children to lean on them too much for support or expect them to make up for adult friends.

3. Learn to switch gear. We have seen that children need a mixture of soft and firm love. In the past, women tended to be good at giving this gentlelove while men's strength was seen in being firm and tough. We know today, however, that men and women are not limited in these ways and that a parent can develop both these sides so as to provide firmness *and* softness when necessary. It is easier to make the switch when you are aware.

4. Find role models for your sons. Most lone parents are women, and the father may have 'disappeared' altogether – although it is usually a great help if contact can be kept with him. But even in two-parent families it is good for boys to have other men in their lives who respect women and who can provide them with models of what it means to be a man. This might include coaches, male schoolteachers, uncles, a grandfather – any man whom you would like your son to be like.

– with your face, your voice, the way you sit or stoop down to the child's level and *look* at her (without staring). A smile or a frown can make all the difference, for the right *words* are of little use if a child senses a lack of interest or understanding in your face or in your tone of voice.

Good listening sometimes means remaining silent. At other times, an understanding grunt or "yes" or "I see" may help. Sometimes it may help to ask a gentle question or tell a similar story from your own experience. Most of the time, however, a question or story can be most unsuitable – if it stops the flow or seems to leave the speaker less open. That is the acid test: is your listening helping your child to talk, to trust, to be more open, to clarify, to feel understood, to make his own decisions?

What is often helpful is to listen beyond the words, beyond the story, beyond the details, to discover the *feelings*, the *person*. And to check out in your own words that you are hearing those feelings correctly. This is called *active* listening.

Active listening.
Active listening is a term used by Dr Thomas Gordon in his book 'Parent Effectiveness Training.' It means grasping what your child is *really* saying, *really* feeling, then playing that feeling back in your own words with understanding and with caring. This is often called 'empathy.' You try to feel what your child is feeling; and you check it out by playing back what you hear. Here is an example.
Joe: I'm finished with Paul! He's mean! And stupid!
Mother: You sound very annoyed with him...
Joe: I hate him!
Mother: It's as strong as that. You're mad with him!
Joe: Yeah. I loaned him my bike and he left it in the mud.
Mother: Oh! Your lovely new bike!

Joe: Yeah. I'm going to have to clean it all up now...

'Active listening' sounds totally unnatural. People just don't talk like that. My children would think something was wrong with me. They would tell me to go and get my head examined.

Active listening may seem artificial and strange at first, but it is not something to be used all the time. Upset or excited children are so anxious to express their feelings that they will not find active listening the slightest bit strange when you use it well. They can feel understood, they can begin to see more clearly what is happening and they can think their way better through a problem. So this kind of listening creates better communication and understanding in a family. It encourages a child to trust, to say more, to talk about difficult areas like feelings, friends, sex, drugs, etc. And it has great power to heal.

We'll look at another example. Ruth has just been told that she may not go to a mid-week disco because of schoolwork.

Ruth: You're always saying no! You hate me, don't you!

Father: You're angry with me because you think I'm not being fair.

Ruth: Fair! You're a dictator. Always laying down the law.

Father: Mm... (*pause*) So you see me just tying you down with rules

Ruth: Yeah! That's right!

Father: And you're fed up with the rules...

Ruth: Yeah. I'm treated like a little four-year-old around here – except that a four-year-old would have more freedom!

Father: Mm... I think you've a sense that I don't trust you.

Ruth: Exactly! You *don't* trust me.

Notice that Ruth's feelings are very strong. This kind of mirror-listening is only to be used when feelings are *strong*, otherwise it would come across as artificial and unreal. Notice too that the father did not use the exact same words as his daughter and that he kept trying to reflect back her *feelings* as well. It may seem that he didn't get far, but he kept calm and allowed Ruth the freedom to express her anger. He may not see immediate results, but Ruth will now be more capable of coming to terms with her problem. Contrast that with what often happens in families and you can see why communication can break down so easily, especially between parents and teenagers.

How to begin.
A good way to begin to use active listening is to become more aware of feelings. You might pay closer attention to what your children say and try to grasp the *feelings* that lie behind their words. Some common feeling words are: afraid, annoyed, angry, anxious, bored, cold, comfortable, confident, delighted, disappointed, disheartened, depressed, disgusted, embarrassed, excited, fed-up, frustrated, furious, glad, grateful, happy, hopeless, hurt, lonely, mad, miserable, over the moon, proud, relaxed, relieved, sad, satisfied, shy, uncomfortable, upset, willing, worried, yucky.

Here are some examples of things children say and (in italics) what they might be feeling beneath the surface:

You don't have to tell me what to do! (*I feel humiliated, small, unimportant.*) I wish I didn't live here! (*I feel angry, mad with you.*) I hate school! (*I feel bored, useless, miserable.*) You call that lovemaking – it sounds disgusting! (*I'm embarrassed, uncomfortable with my own body.*) I can't sleep. (*I feel tense, upset, confused.*)

When your child's feelings seem clear, you might try reflecting that feeling back, "You feel..." "You're very..." "You seem to be..." "Sounds as if you're..." The aim is to allow your child to open up and say more. So try not to reflect back the feeling stronger or weaker than it is. Otherwise, a child may close up again.

IF YOU HAVE A PARTNER...

There is an old saying that the best thing a couple can do for their children is to love each other, and studies are now confirming that children tend to be happier when you are close and affectionate as a couple. If you have a partner, your children have a lot to gain when you invest time in her or him.

One strong recommendation from experts is that you spend 10-20 minutes each day, preferably after work, listening and unwinding together and catching up on one another. Let the children know that they are not allowed to interrupt your time together except for emergencies. (This is explained more fully in our book *Couple Alive*.)

Children will often test you to see if they can play one of you off against the other but at a deeper level they *like* it when you make time for each other and make it clear that the two of you come first. This is so important to them that they are happier with a lone parent than with a couple who are constantly bickering – though they also benefit when the lone parent has a close friendship with another adult.

You can listen too much!

We saw that active listening must not be overdone – it will not help when it is used at the wrong times. When your son is constantly moaning and looking for sympathy, that is a bad habit, he is merely trying to hook you in, and more listening will not help. When your daughter complains that her brother has got a bigger helping of dinner, it may be better to say something humorous: "Yes, dear, we like him more than we like you!" Used at the appropriate time, however, active listening is one of the most powerful skills a parent can have.

Summing up

To sum up. When a child is upset about his broken toy, or depressed because she has no friends, what that child may need most is *listening*, a sense of being *understood*. Unfortunately, parents often think it is their duty to come up with solutions. Whereas listening with understanding is actually the *beginning* of the solution and often the *only* solution that is needed.

You might begin to practise active listening with these four stages:

1. Listen for feelings.

2. Try to put a name on the feeling.

3. Check out with your child if you are right.

4. Let the child clarify or correct you if you've got the feeling wrong.

It will take time to learn and be at ease with this new skill. It will feel awkward at first, but with practice and patience it soon becomes natural.

Active listening is only for special occasions when a child's feelings are strong. But there are many opportunities in the course of a day when we might slow down or stop trying to argue back, make a switch and listen with attention and interest. Good listening is much more than a mere technique or skill for it is one of the most effective ways to show genuine concern and under-standing and give children the 'gentlelove' that is so good for their growth in confidence and love.

When I've listened well, I've seen Tom change from being depressed and hopeless about things. He didn't need me to tell him what to do – he was able to work it out for himself.

GETTING IN TOUCH

For each of the children's comments below decide what parents usually say

that is not helpful. Then ask yourself what the child might really be thinking and feeling.

'Robert has all new label clothes.'
'You don't care about me!'
'Our maths teacher is stupid!'
'You don't have to go on about it!'
'Tom's lucky he's the youngest!'

PLANS FOR NEXT WEEK

1. To which child will you give a good experience of being listened to and understood this week? What would be a *natural* time for that? (Over a special supper? Bedtime? When a child is upset?) How will you begin? What might help your child to talk more freely and to say more? You may like to write down what you plan.

2. If you have a partner, consider setting aside at least 10 minutes a day, taking turns to listen and catch up on one another. Remember that all these skills work with adults as well!

Plans..._____

Please read chapter five of this handbook before the next session

TABLE 4: LISTENING

Consider the following examples of helpful and unhelpful responses to what children say. The examples given in the 'Helpful listening' column show the **attitude** *of the parents rather than the actual words they might use – the words will vary according to the situation.*

Child says:	Non-listening approach	Helpful listening
1. You don't have to tell me what to do.	Oh, yes I do – I'm your father and you'll do what you're told.	You hate me telling you what to do – it makes you angry…
2. I hate Margaret. I'm not going to play with her anymore!	You mustn't hate people, dear. I'm sure she didn't mean it!	Mm... Sounds like you're upset with her...
3. I'm just no good at maths.	Well, you'll just have to keep trying.	You feel kind of hopeless about maths... That's really hard…
4. Why can't I go too! She's only a year older than me.	That's enough. We're not going to talk any more about it!	You're feeling a bit cheated – it doesn't seem fair to you.
5. Our team won, Mum!	That's good! Now go and wash you hands.	Oh! You must be delighted!
6. The arm of my new doll is smashed. (*child crying*).	Don't worry, love, I'll buy you a new one.	(Hug) And you were so pleased with your new doll. That's *so* upsetting!

CASE STUDIES

Read the following conversations (it may be better if two or three people read them aloud). Then, in groups of three, discuss the questions at the end of each situation.

LUCY (9): I've nothing to do! I called for Sheila but she's gone on holidays.
FATHER: Oh well, you can always get someone else to play with you.
What feelings might Lucy have had when she arrived home? If you were Lucy, what effect might your father's remark have had on you? How could he use active listening to show understanding instead?

PAT (12): I hate my teacher. He's the meanest man I've ever met. I wish he was dead!
MOTHER: That's no way to talk about anyone! You must have been doing something wrong if he's down on you.
How do you think Pat may have been feeling about himself and his school and his teacher? If you were Pat, what effect might your mother's remark have had on you? How could she use active listening and help him express some of his feelings?

DAVID (5, close to tears): Richard and Joe sent me away. They said I'm too small to play with them.
MOTHER: Don't worry, David. You're better off without friends like that!
If you were David, how would you feel if your friends had treated you in this way? What effect might his mother's remark have had on him? What might have helped instead? A hug? A listening ear? How might she use active listening?

10-year-old Tom has been at his homework for over half an hour.
TOM: This homework is too difficult for me. I give up.
MOTHER: Well, you can't afford to give up. You just haven't stuck at it long enough. You need to keep trying.
How do you think Tom feels about his homework? If you were Tom, what effect might your mother's remark have had on you? How can she use active listening to help him express some of his feelings?

ANNA (15): Dad, guess what! Mike has asked me to go to the disco!
FATHER: Well you just make sure you're in before one o'clock!
How do you think Anna feels about her date? What effect might her father's remark have on her? And how might he use active listening instead?

CHAPTER 5 – COMMUNICATING ABOUT PROBLEMS

Vincent (13) had just had a snack but had not cleared up after himself. When his mother saw the mess, she felt like screaming at him to clear it up. She wanted to tell him she was not his maid and to remind him of how often she had told him to clear things away. Instead, she calmed herself, called him, and said, "Vincent, I've spent a long time cleaning the kitchen, and when you leave it like this I feel discouraged." Vincent said he was sorry and cleaned it up right away. The mother's approach had worked because she had used what Dr Thomas Gordon calls an 'I' message. **With 'I' messages parents tell their children as honestly and calmly as possible how they feel.** Let's look at another example.

Father and mother were having a sleep-in on Saturday morning. At five thirty, Jacqueline (5), came into her parents' room, woke up her father and wanted to 'play.' Father wanted to scold her crossly, "What do you mean by wakening me up! Couldn't you see I was asleep! Now get out of this room and stop being a little nuisance." Instead, he decided to give Jacqueline an 'I'

message, "Jackie, I'm feeling sleepy and tired – much too sleepy to play with you. It's very early, but if you want to play, you can play with toys in your room." Reluctantly, Jacqueline went back to her room. She wasn't pleased, but at least she hadn't suffered an explosion from her father. Telling her his feelings had helped.

Who owns the problem?
In the last chapter, we saw how active listening can help when a child has a problem. In the same way, an 'I' message can help when a *parent* has a problem. It is important, then, to be clear about who *owns* a problem – the parent, or the child, or both? When Vincent left the kitchen in a mess, Vincent himself may have been quite *happy*. His mother was not happy about it, so she owned the problem – the untidy kitchen was upsetting to her and was interfering with her rights. On the other hand, if Vincent is upset because he has no friends, his mother can 'help' him much more effectively when she first of all recognises that it is *Vincent* who owns

WHEN THERE IS DIVORCE...

A quarter of all divorces in Britain involve children aged 11-15. Parents are often so caught up with their own distress during the break-up period that the children's needs tend to be neglected. And things get worse, not better, if a parent enters too quickly into a new relationship instead of living with the pain for a while. It is important to talk with a counsellor or other adult about the pain rather than bottle it up or offload feelings on to your children.

The greatest stress for young people is their sense of guilt, thinking that they are the *cause* of the separation. They often express this in anger at the parent with whom they are left. There is usually a drop in their performance at school and teenagers tend to use tobacco and drugs more – and to leave home and become parents earlier.

There is a great need for ongoing talking and listening, reassuring young people that they are not at fault and that you still love them. You cannot take away the pain divorce causes, but you can *lessen* the ill effects by:

1.) maintaining contact between your former partner and your children – it helps if you can arrange to live reasonably close.

2.) refusing to use your children in any warring with the ex-partner. It is good for them when ex-partners can continue to communicate and show respect.

this problem. This is an important distinction, because it happens quite often that we take on our *children's*

problems as if they were their own – and that doesn't help either of us.

Before we go back to have a look at 'I' messages in more detail, let's look at how we can help children deal with problems that *they* own.

When the child owns the problem

What do parents usually do when their children have problems? Sometimes they criticise the child, lecturing, scolding and pointing out mistakes, "I can't trust you to stay out of trouble!" Other parents show more understanding, taking the child aside and offering advice. But many children have a built-in resistance to their parents' advice. Besides, offering advice or solving children's problems for them doesn't help them to take responsibility for *themselves*. We need to give advice at times, but it is best, when possible, to work with children in helping them find their *own* solutions.

Part of this is helping young people to *talk* about feelings instead of *acting* on them. At times, you will need to interrupt your daughter's 'helpless' moaning or whining and insist that she *tell* the other person what she wants. At times, you might cut through your son's sulking and grumpy mood by leaving the room, saying, "I'd like to help. Come and talk with me when you know what you want." At other times, you might use active listening to help a child talk through what has been happening, "I'm wondering why you threw a stone at him? Were you just bored or were you angry at the time?" "Did you think of telling him you were angry?" "How do you feel now about what you did?" "What will you do in future?" **We must not be afraid to challenge children's behaviour at all ages and to help them think about how they are acting and how it affects others.**

We also need to set clear boundaries. For instance, we might impose a consequence for hitting or kicking, "In future, you'll have to do a chore for the person you hit – hitting is just not on in this family!"

STEP-FAMILIES

There are over two and a half million children in stepfamilies in Britain and it is estimated that stepfamilies will soon outnumber birth families.

Adding even one new person to a family can be a big challenge, so you can see how blending two families can cause tension. Children who may still be suffering from the loss of one parent may feel threatened by a new 'rival' for their parent's attention and affection. Meanwhile, the new arrival may feel hurt at the sense of rejection by stepchildren – and guilty for not having warm feelings towards them. It is not surprising that more second marriages end up in divorce than first marriages and that children tend to do better in lone-parent families or in families where a parent has died rather than divorced.

There are many success stories, however, when the adults are prepared for the tensions and willing to be patient in building a relationship with a stepchild. A stepparent needs to allow for the natural parent to spend considerable time with the children. It is also good to be clear that the natural parent is the one who is *responsible* for parenting them.

Four stages for older children
As children get older, the four stages below have been found useful in helping them talk through their problems:

1. Start with active listening. This helps your child to feel understood – and to understand the situation more clearly, "You're very worried about the exams..."

2. Begin together to think up possible solutions. (This is called brainstorming.) "What would you like to see happening?" "What do you think you might be able to do about this?" Try to get a number of different ideas, and chip in yourself, saying what *you* would like to see happening. It is surprising how many possibilities two people can come up with when they put their minds to it. It usually helps to write the ideas down.

3. Help your child to choose one idea. It is best not to tell your children the snags you see in their suggestions. Try instead to help them with gentle questions to see for themselves what the snags and advantages are, "Which of these ideas seems best to you?" "When will you do this?" "For how long?" When one idea emerges that seems satisfactory, it often helps to write the decisions on paper.

4. Fix a time for reviewing how the plan is working. Solving problems may be a waste of time if you don't also make time to look back and see how the solution is working out in practice. "When will we get together again to see how things are going?"

These four stages apply if the *child* owns the problem. They may be time-consuming, but a lot of good 'connecting' and parenting happens in the process.

Needless to say, insisting that children talk out problems instead of acting them out will make little sense if *you* don't talk out *your* anger instead of acting it out! And that brings us to what happens when it is the *parent* who owns the problem.

When you own the problem
When parents have problems with their children, they often correct them with 'you' messages. "You've left the door open!" "You didn't clean the mud off your shoes!" "You've taken too much milk." Even if the parent does not add something more insulting, a child can easily feel humiliated and attacked by their remarks – and by the tone of voice used. So 'you' messages are not respectful or effective. Parents need to be able to speak about their annoyance or frustration in such a way that there are no winners or losers.

'I' messages help us to be effective. Unlike 'you' messages, they do not blame. They say truthfully, but not aggressively, how we feel about the result of a child's behaviour. Here are some more examples: "When you take a lot of milk, I feel annoyed that there isn't enough left to go round." "When we agree together on a bedtime and then you stay up late, I feel a bit lost because I don't know where we stand with each other any more." "When you leave your things scattered over the dining-room floor, I feel ashamed to take people in."

'I' messages will solve *some* problems – not all of them. Action, as we'll see, is often called for as well. The point is that an 'I' message (not moaning, not blaming, not critical) shows respect for a child and can be the *beginning* of a solution. Even a simple statement of feelings like: "I'm just in rotten form today" is so much more helpful than acting out feelings, blaming and making your child feel guilty and bad.

She knew she was in the wrong and she was bristling as she got ready for my usual attack. Instead, I said, "Ann, when you stay out so late, I get frightened that something has happened to you." It was a more civilised approach, and you could see her softening.

Giving 'I' messages.

Have you noticed in the examples we've given that the emphasis is not so much on the behaviour you don't like but on it's *effects*? Focusing on the effects usually works best. That is why an 'I' message is usually expressed something like this: "When... I feel... because..." "*When* you play your music so loud, *I feel* deafened and annoyed *because* this is my space too."

'I' messages may not work for you. This may be because you use them too often, or because your tone of voice is aggressive – or because you begin with 'I feel' and then give a strong 'you' message that does not mention feelings, "I feel you're just bullying your little brother!" We have to be careful to express *feelings* and avoid blaming. For this reason it is sometimes best not to speak about very angry feelings but to

tell your child instead about the hurt, embarrassment or disappointment linked with your anger, "I feel *embarrassed* when my friends come in and you don't speak to them, because I want them to feel welcome.'

It also helps to give your children 'I' messages about your positive feelings, "I'm delighted with the job you did in the backyard – it's so much nicer to go out there when it's tidy." **Perhaps the two most important and powerful 'I' messages of all are, "I love you," and "I'm sorry – will you forgive me?"**

Jackie, I'm feeling much too sleepy and tired to play with you.

The two approaches.

Let's sum up then. This chapter deals with situations where you or your children have problems – about disrespect, bedtimes, pocket money, chores, watching TV, unsuitable friends, blaring music, etc., etc. There are two different approaches, depending on who owns the problem. So it helps to start by asking yourself, "Who owns this problem – me or my child?"

If *you* own the problem, ask, "What are the effects of this behaviour, and how do I honestly feel about them?" Then give an 'I' message, saying how you feel about these effects. This shows respect for a child, but you need to be careful not to over-use it.

If your child owns the problem, it will usually help to use active listening. For serious problems you may need to withdraw from the conflict and suggest a time for talking things through. The four steps for problem management can then be followed. (If your children are still too young to use these four stages, you may like to *practise* using them with a partner. Many couples find these four stages help them to deal well with tensions in their own lives.)

Talking a problem through like this is not always enough. Action is often needed as well. In the next chapter, we will look at suitable action that can be taken, but it is always good to straighten out the lines of communication first.

GETTING IN TOUCH

See if you can decide who owns each of the following problems – the parent or the child. (To decide who owns a problem, it usually helps to ask, "Who is most unhappy or upset in this situation?" Parents sometimes allow **themselves** to get upset when it is their **child** who owns the problem, but this guideline should work for you most of the time.)

1. Child dilly-dallies over dressing and breakfast – then doesn't do chore.
2. In spite of being called, your 12-year-old daughter has slept in and is now late for school.
3. Your 6-year-old child begins to climb a ladder.
4. Your child is disrespectful to you in front of neighbours.
5. Your 5-year-old and 7-year-old are constantly squabbling and fighting.
6. Your son is bullying a neighbour's child.
7. Homework is untidy or not being done at all.
8. Bedtimes are being ignored.
9. Your teenager is drifting with the crowd and not working at school.

PLANS FOR NEXT WEEK

1. This week set aside time with one child to go through the four stages for managing a problem. Which child? What would be a good problem to start with? When will you do this? You may like to write down what you plan.

2. Try giving one clear, well-thought-out 'I' message to someone each day for the next week – you'll only get better by practising.

3. The four stages for managing problems also work with the *adults* in your life. How do you feel about trying them with a partner?

Plans..._____

_____

Please read chapter six of this handbook before the next session

TABLE 5: COMMUNICATING ABOUT PROBLEMS

*This Table shows the two different approaches parents can take, depending on who owns a problem. Sometimes a problem belongs to both parent and child, but it is usually obvious who **most** owns it.*

Problem	Who owns it?	Caution	Active Listening	'I' message
1. Child regularly leaves door open.	Parent	Try not to blame – focus on *results* of door being left open.		"I'm frustrated that you've left the door open – I'm left sitting in a draught."
2. Child crying because older brother called her names.	Child	It usually does not help to interfere in squabbles except in cases of danger.	(*Hug*) "You're terribly upset..."	
3. Seven-year-old is trying to cut bread with a sharp knife.	Parent	Best not to panic. Watch tone of voice – alarm creates alarm and nervousness.		(*Calmly*) "When you use the sharp knife, I feel nervous in case you cut yourself."
4. Child has been ignored by a friend.	Child	It doesn't help to pretend it doesn't matter – nor to 'solve' the child's problem.	"You're feeling angry and hurt..."	
5. Child leaves your tools out in the rain.	Parent	It is best if you can avoid scolding or criticising.		"I feel annoyed when the tools are left outside – I don't want them to get rusty or lost or stolen."
6. Child hates school.	Child	Be slow to advise – it probably won't help.	"You're feeling useless and lost at school..."	

CASE STUDIES

Form groups of three and discuss the situations below. In each case, decide who owns the problem – the parent or the child. If the child owns the problem, see how you might use active listening and show understanding without taking over the problem. If the parent owns the problem, see if you can give a suitable 'I' message to communicate how you feel. (This is just for practice – it is obviously not appropriate to use active listening every time a child has a problem – nor to use 'I' messages every time *you* have a problem!)

- You're trying to have a chat with a neighbour who seldom calls and who is quite lonely, but your 6-year-old daughter keeps interrupting you.
- 11-year-old Mark was going down town on his bicycle. A minute later, he comes back to the house looking fed-up. "Ah, dad," he says, "Guess what! My front wheel's punctured! What am I going to do?"
- Mother is about to make the dinner when she finds that her 5-year-old has left toys scattered all over the kitchen floor.
- Your 15-year-old daughter, Elizabeth, comes in, looking pale. She announces that she has just failed an important exam.

Here is a shortened version of what can happen with skilled use of the four stages of problem solving. Can you pick out each of the four stages as the mother uses them? (It may help if you look at the four stages in chapter five.)

Jeremy: (*Slams door.*) There's far too much work in this house. Tidy your room! Clear the table! Sweep the floor! Wash the dishes! I hate living here!

Mother: Seems like a lot of work, Jeremy. Makes you fed up...

Jeremy: Yeah. Other boys don't have to do anything at home!

Mother: So that leaves you feeling a bit cheated – like it's a real burden for you.

Jeremy: Yeah, that's right. But it never stops!

Mother: So what do you think you could do about it?

Jeremy: There's nothing *I* can do about it. *I* don't make the decisions – you do!

Mother: Well, if you could decide, what would be a fair thing to do?

Jeremy: (*uncooperatively*) Well, you're the grown-ups. *You* should do the work.

Mother: That's one possibility. Anything else that might be fair.

Jeremy: Pay someone to come in and do the work.

Mother: That's two suggestions. Any more?

Jeremy: You could at least share out jobs so one person doesn't end up doing so much.

Mother: Mm. That's three things we might do. Dad and I do the jobs. Pay someone else to do them. Or share them out in the family. Which idea do you think is best?

Jeremy (*softening*): Well, the first two ideas are the easiest... But it really wouldn't be fair to you and Dad. (*pause*) *Could* we pay someone?

Mother: We couldn't afford that... So where does that leave us?

Jeremy: Share out the jobs, I suppose.

Mother: Are you willing to do your share?

Jeremy: As long as my job isn't going to take too long. What would I have to do?

Mother: What would you prefer to do?

Jeremy: Mm... I'd rather do the chores at the weekend.

Mother: Right. But I don't want to be running around after you reminding you. Are you sure you're prepared to do this?

Jeremy: Look, would I say it if I wasn't prepared to do it!

Mother: Okay. Let's write down what you have to do and we'll try it for a week to see then how it works. Okay?

Jeremy: Okay.

CHAPTER 6: DISCIPLINING CHILDREN

Patrick (14) was sitting with his feet on the couch, reading a magazine. His mother decided to give him an 'I' message, since this was obviously her problem.

"Patrick, it annoys me when you put your feet up on the couch – it's quite new and I don't want it to get dirty."

Patrick merely grunted, "I like sitting this way," and continued to read.

"Patrick, either sit properly on the couch or sit any way you like on the floor. Which do you want to do?"

He scowled, but he put his feet on the floor and sat back on the couch. His mother had treated him with respect by giving him an 'I' message, but when that had not worked, she offered him a limited choice. She did not scold, nag, threaten, punish or coax – but she had used an effective 'firmlove' method of discipline.

Learning from consequences.
We have already seen that successful parenting rests on the twin foundations of gentlelove and firmlove. In this chapter, we want to look more closely at firmlove – being able to say 'no' and set clear limits while remaining loving, not shouting and not getting angry.

In the past, children were often disciplined by punishment or reward – which tended to work only in the short term. The emphasis today is on *inner* discipline, on helping children to take responsibility for their *own* behaviour rather than always be looking over their shoulders to see if we approve. **One good way for them to learn this self-discipline is when we give them a limited choice and let them live with the consequences of what they choose.**

There will be times when you *cannot* let them choose, for example when you consider something is dangerous for them. When you have to say 'no,' it is important to give a reason (not more than one reason or they won't hear you!) and to say it firmly. It is not the end of the world if you fall back on "No, because I'm your father and I think this is best for you!" *Constantly* forcing them to do things your way, however, may only encourage them to rebel.

When you do give children a limited choice, it is important not to be half-hearted or apologetic. Let your son know

48

this is serious by looking him straight in the eye and saying, "If you hit her again, you won't be allowed to play in this room for the rest of the day. So you have a choice. Do you understand this?" Wait for a reply. They may attempt to argue in order to hook you in and buy time, but this is not the time to reason with your child. (Breathing more deeply will usually help you to stay calm and strong.)

Having said what the consequence will be, it is essential to follow through on it. Children like to know how real the limits are, so they will test your firmness. When they fight back at you, throw tantrums, or shout, "I hate you," do not panic and back down, afraid that you are frustrating the child. Frustration is part of life and part of learning. **Children need limits and feel happier and more secure when you are firm and not just making idle threats.** Have you noticed what happens if you weaken and give in? Your child still remains miserable! And the misbehaviour and lack of self-discipline get worse. Giving in 'for the sake of peace' is only storing up problems for the future: it will not bring peace.

Allowing children to choose.
In helping children learn to discipline themselves, then, we need to give them increasing opportunities to make their own decisions. Instead of lecturing, nagging or punishing them, we might simply offer a choice, "I hate all this squabbling at the table. I want you to stop it now or else go to your room – which do you want to do?" If your two small children continue to squabble, you again offer a choice, "I see you've chosen to leave the table. Do you want to go to your room by yourselves or would you prefer me to carry you?" They will usually keep their dignity by choosing to leave the room themselves. If there is no answer, however, you might gently carry both children out of the room, assuring them, "You're welcome to come back in when you

have decided to settle down." You are still offering them choices and treating them with respect. **They learn a great deal in a short time when they have to live with the consequences of their choices.** If they choose not to eat at a mealtime and you refuse to let them snack to make up for it, they will feel a little hunger until the next meal. Or if they refuse to wear coats, they may feel cold and may learn from that experience.

Here is another example. Twelve-year-old George lies on in the morning and keeps everyone late for school. So you decide with the other children on a suitable time to leave and then you announce, "Okay, from now on, the car will leave at that time. Anyone who is not ready will have to walk to school and accept the consequences of dealing with the teacher. Is that agreed?" Be flexible enough to allow for genuine emer-gencies, but you need to be firm in sticking to what you promised. You will probably be the one who finds this hardest because you want to be liked or because you feel guilty, so you need to remind yourself that .you are doing this out of love for your child. This is positive parenting. How will children learn to say 'no' to drugs or whatever if they never hear it from you?

_____

I find a good way to break the deadlock when they won't make a choice is to give them another choice – 'if you can't decide soon, I'll decide for you.'

_____

Using consequences is not a method of punishment.
When parents discipline their children by using consequences, it is best if these consequences flow naturally or logically out of the situation. If Jack breaks a window, it may follow logically that he has to pay towards a new one, but it would make less sense to stop his pocket money if he does not keep his room tidy, as there is no logical connection between money and room tidiness. Instead, you

might say, "I've just vacuumed the house, but there were a lot of things on your floor, so I'll leave the vacuum cleaner here for you to do it." Jack then has to live with the *real* consequences of keeping his room untidy. Or when Anna has agreed to go to bed at 10 o'clock but breaks her agreement, you might say, "For the next two days we'll go back to the old arrangement of bedtime at 9.30, Anna. Then we'll try the 10 o'clock agreement again." Notice that there isn't any hint of punishment, and the possibility of a new start is always presented. It generally helps to say something like, "You can try again tomorrow." Reminding them of a fresh start avoids humiliating them and can help *you* to stay friendly.

There are other ways to make sure that consequences are not seen as punishment: not reminding, threatening, warning, getting angry or saying something like, "Maybe this will teach you!" **Your firmness in following through on the consequence is much more effective than talking.**

Firmlove is not cold. It is both kind and strong, gentle and firm, flowing out of your desire for what is best for the child, not out of your anger. So you might even invite a young child, "Let's clear up this mess together," rather than always give a choice. After all, the *purpose* of using consequences is to help children make responsible decisions – not to force them to do your will. So it helps if you can involve your children in *making* the decision too (about bedtime, about which chores to do, etc.)

Speaking positively
The whole thrust of using consequences, then, is a positive one. Instead of always saying "don't," you may like to offer the choice by saying "If..." Instead of "Don't cut the bread on the tablecloth," try, "If you want to cut the bread, please use the breadboard."

Another way of offering choices positively is to use what we might call the 'as soon as' method to deal with requests and demands. "Yes, you can go out to play as soon as the dishes are washed and dried," "Yes, you may watch television as soon as you've tidied your bedroom." "Yes, you can have the dessert as soon as you've eaten your dinner," "I'm putting the bike away now, but you can use it again as soon as you come to an agreement about it that will stop the squabbling." In these instances, the child is really being given a choice. You are not insisting on the dinner being eaten: you are allowing the child to choose and to live with the consequences of not eating it. At the same time, you are speaking positively. It is better to say, "You can read your comic as soon as you've vacuumed the floor" than to say, "No, you can't read your comic. You haven't vacuumed the floor!"

Your own behaviour can also offer a positive lesson in discipline. It is easier to convince children that they must not shout or hit if you *talk* about your anger instead of *acting* on it.

"I can't think up consequences!"
"That's all very well," you may protest, "but most of the time I can't *think* of a consequence, so I fall back on my old ways of threatening or making snap decisions."

One useful tip is to postpone making a decision and to withdraw from the conflict, especially when there is a lot of tension between you and your child. That gives you a chance to think.

Another tip is to ask children themselves about the consequences of their actions, "What do you think we can do about this?" That gives them a sense of being *involved* in solving the problem. When Jim loses your saw, you don't necessarily have to think of a consequence yourself. You could ask, "How are you going to get me a new saw, Jim?" When children have just had a row, you might ask, "I wonder what other things you could have done to each other instead of hitting and using violence when you were so angry?" In this way, their options are widened.

In the last analysis, however, it is not a disaster if we sometimes end up imposing consequences that do not flow logically out of the situation, if we ground children or deprive them of the phone, TV or the computer. None of us is a super-parent!

What about 'time out'?
In recent years, 'time out' has become a popular method of discipline. Properly understood, it can be an effective way of offering a choice and allowing children to learn from consequences. You start by explaining to your children what will happen when they misbehave in future. They will be told to stand facing into the corner in order *to cool down and think*. It is not punishment – just a chance to think without distractions. As soon as they are ready to talk about what happened, they can choose to come back to you. You will then ask them what they did wrong and what they are going to do in future.

The younger children are when this method is started, the easier it is to introduce (though they may need to be *held* facing the wall to begin with). But it must not be used as a form of punishment – Steve Biddulph uses the term 'stand and think' rather than 'time out' to emphasise its positive nature. With older children, too, we have to be more flexible, and the 'standing and thinking' does not have to be done facing a wall. But it is an excellent way of dealing with the rudeness, put-downs and disrespect that have become so common today. It helps children to become more responsible and sensitive to how their actions affect others. And when it is done properly, it creates better connection between parents and children and everyone feels better. (This method is explained more fully in *More secrets of Happy Children* – see reading list.)

Staying firm.
Applying consequences requires a certain firmness and strength (but not harshness) from parents. Neighbours and friends, even teachers, sometimes expect you to be a 'good' parent rather than a responsible one; they may criticise you for not making sure that your children arrive at school on time (though it can help to have a word with the teacher about what you are doing). You may also feel guilty if your children dilly-dally and don't make their lunches in time some day, then have to rush off to school without a lunch. But staying firm and not bailing a child out too readily is crucial. Adults learn all the time from consequences – if we go to the shop without money or forget to buy something in the supermarket. So these are excellent opportunities for children to learn to be responsible.

Using consequences is only *one* method of discipline – all the other skills of this course are also closely linked to discipline. But *some* form of discipline is essential. 'Spoilt' children who are given their own way and get everything they ask for can become their own worst enemies. Lack of limits can leave them feeling insecure and unsure of boundaries. Worst of all, not having limits around misbehaviour can actually prevent them from testing out and discovering who they are – which Eric Erikson has highlighted as the most important life-task of teenagers! Limits are that important.

buying shoes for six-year-old David

HOW CHILDREN EAT

Science has now shown what people have suspected for some time – that there is a clear link between how children eat and how they behave, including how they perform at school. Foods with high sugar content tend to give a burst of high energy (which can leave a child hyperactive and lead to behaviour problems) followed by a quick loss of energy and concentration. If they must have junk food, it may be best to keep it for *after* a proper meal.

Before leaving home in the morning, we eat our most important meal. Children need a breakfast that will give them energy for the day. What they eat early in the day is much better than a big meal in the evening because a good breakfast gets burned up when it is used for mental and physical work instead of being stored in the body as fat.

It may be important to introduce changes in diet gradually, however, for glamorous media images have already made children as young as eight over-conscious of food, and these images are partly responsible for the growth in eating disorders like anorexia and bulimia. If your child wants to lose weight, offer sensible advice – take more exercise, avoid fatty or fried foods, eat plenty of fresh fruit and vegetables – and make breakfast your main meal!

If an eating disorder develops, try to deal with it early – contact your GP as soon as possible (the sooner your teen gets help, the quicker the recovery can be). The quality of help varies, so it may also help to contact the Eating Disorders Association Helpline at 01603-621414.

I like to stay flexible. If some children want to read until eleven and can still get up fresh in the morning, isn't that okay? I think the very best kind of limits for them is bumping up against a parent who is a real person with values and feelings and can say, "I'm angry that you're so tired this morning because you didn't get to bed on time."

Do your best, then, to stay firm in keeping to your side of an agreement rather than make idle threats. If you agree to have your evening meal at six and your son doesn't arrive until six thirty, you will hardly be helping him if you prepare an extra meal instead of expecting him to rustle something up for himself.

Examples of consequences.
Here, then, are some more examples of how parents can foster good discipline by using consequences.

Mother is buying shoes for six-year-old David. He has taken a fancy to sandals instead. When she tells him they are not suitable, he throws a tantrum. This is a power-struggle and he is testing his strength against hers, sensing how embarrassing his misbehaviour in public can be. She does not give in, however. She leaves the shoe shop and he has to do without new shoes for a few days. She does not scold. She explains that they can go back to the shop when he is prepared to behave. Even young children understand consequences quickly.

Nancy is eight. She finds excuses to get out of bed after being settled each evening. So her father makes sure she has been to the toilet, etc., then announces, "If you get up again, I'll turn off the night-light in the hallway to help you sleep. You decide." When she gets up again, father turns off the light, saying, "I'm turning off the light, but we'll try again tomorrow." She cries to see if her father will change his mind, but he refuses to let himself be manipulated by her tears. He allows her to learn from the consequences of her own behaviour. (But he listens to what Nancy has to say through her tears – that may sometimes reveal an underlying worry.)

Eleven-year-old Martin is invited to a birthday party and his parents say he can go if he has done his chores. When the time comes, he has not done the chores but pleads to be allowed to go. His parents refuse gently but firmly. When he continues to plead, they leave the room.

Deirdre (12) does not want to go to school – she says she is not feeling well (though she may be foxing). Her father is sympathetic but insists that if she stays home from school she must spend the day in bed (with no TV) since she is ill. She then makes her own choice.

Robert (11) and Edward (13) are fighting in the car. Their mother stops the car and explains, "I find it impossible to drive while this fighting is going on. I want you to settle down or else to leave the car and walk home. Which do you want to do?" This is not a threat. She accepts their decision, either way. It is surprising how quickly children get the message.

Fifteen-year-old Becky thumps her younger brother when she is angry with him. Her mother says, "Becky, I would be failing you as a parent if I didn't help you learn to deal with your anger. In future, this house is a no-hitting zone. Every time anyone hits or kicks, they will have to do a chore for the person they hit. Do you understand this?" From then on, Becky's mother follows through on this.

All these are examples of *possible* ways of using consequences, though there are many *other* possibilities in the same situations. What they all have in common is *action with little talking*. Applying consequences in these ways is an effective, non-violent method of dealing with the constant discipline problems that affect every family. Properly understood, this is also a method that is deeply respectful to children.

Summing up

In this book we have met a number of ways of helping children learn to discipline themselves – taking time to train them for new responsibilities, talking things out, encouraging, etc. In this chapter we see that consequences can also be effective. In applying consequences:

1. It helps to offer a choice – this avoids backing children into a corner.

2. Be firm but don't scold. Look your child straight in the eye, mean what you say and do *allow* her to live with the consequence.

3. Stay friendly. Remind your child "You can try again tomorrow," or "I'll come back and talk with you when you've stopped shouting and we've both calmed down."

Using consequences is not a method of punishment but a way of helping children learn from the choices they make. (If they are *not* becoming more responsible or learning self-discipline, we need to consider a different approach.) **It is important that we act out of *love*, thinking of a child's best interests, and that we remember to use the other skills of a responsible parent – children particularly need lots of gentlelove and fun in between the 'disciplining' times.** The foundation for good discipline is laid when they know that they are valued and loved.

Using consequences wasn't good for John and me. It made me a bit cold and removed – and I think he saw it as punishment. I think you have to be careful about how you introduce consequences with a teenager.

GETTING IN TOUCH

What do parents normally do or say when a child...

1. throws a tantrum at home?
2. throws a tantrum in public?
3. won't get up in the morning?
4. watches TV instead of doing homework?
5. stays out an hour later than permitted?
6. refuses to co-operate with the family, do chores, etc.?
7. dresses in what seems to be an outlandish (or careless) way?
8. teases or bullies a little sister?
9. is squabbling with another child?
10. keeps her room very untidy?

PLANS FOR NEXT WEEK

1. Think of one ongoing discipline problem in your home. How could you begin to deal with it, applying consequences? What would be a good time for talking it out with your child? How could you present it as a choice rather than as a punishment or an ultimatum? You may like to write down what you plan.

2. It is easier to discipline children when we are consistent and show some willingness to discipline *ourselves*. Would you like to plan something to improve your own *self*-discipline – in diet, exercise, alcohol, use of the phone...?

Plans..._____

Please read chapter seven of this handbook before the next session

TABLE 6: APPLYING CONSEQUENCES

This table shows ways of allowing children to learn from the consequences of their choices. Can you see how these ideas might apply in your own family?

Problem	Usual Method of Discipline	Using Consequences	Effect
1. Child not getting up when called.	Shout, nag, threaten, keep reminding, coax, force.	Call only once (or give older child alarm clock and allow to be late for school or do without breakfast, if necessary).	Child begins to take responsibility for self in the mornings.
2. Child continually forgets things.	Remind, nag, scold, search, rescue.	Let child experience consequences of forgetting lunch, schoolbooks, etc. For matters that affect parent, work out an agreed consequence in advance – and apply it.	Child quickly learns to take responsibility for remembering.
3. Hair and clothes styles not suitable.	Parent buys child's clothes, decides length of hair, etc.	Allow child greater say in choosing hairstyle and selecting clothes within reasonable limits. Allow child to get wet or cold (within reason) rather than *insist* on appropriate clothes. For going out *together* insist on your rights – that child be suitably dressed – or leave child behind (if necessary with baby-sitter).	Child learns to choose and make decisions about style and about appropriate clothes.
4. Child doesn't brush teeth.	Remind, scold, shame, force.	Offer choice between brushing teeth and giving up sweet things.	Child brushes teeth – and sees link with dental decay.
5. Chores being ignored.	Remind, nag, shout, pay - or parent does chore.	Agree on family chores together. Establish clear consequences for not doing chores.	Children learn to contribute to smooth running of the home.
6. Bedtimes being ignored.	Remind, nag, have a row, force, punish.	Agree together on a bedtime. If ignored, go back for two days to the earlier bedtime, then try again. For younger children, offer choice – to go to bed or be carried to bed. Repeat as often as child gets up.	Child begins to take responsibility for *own* bedtime.
7. Homework not being done.	Scold, warn, lecture, or do homework for child.	Take an interest in the homework, ask questions about it and give *necessary* assistance. But let child face consequences from the *teacher* for poor or no homework.	Child takes responsibility for it *and* develops relationship with parent.

CASE STUDIES

Here are a number of situations that cause problems for parents. Form threes and see if you can decide 1.) How do parents usually deal with these situations? 2.) How might you apply consequences while remaining friendly?

Twelve-year-old Bob has a habit of forgetting to take things to school with him – sometimes his lunch, sometimes his schoolbag, sometimes his coat. His mother has to put herself to a lot of trouble to get these to him. Each time, she lectures and scolds, and every morning she reminds him to check that he has everything with him. Bob still forgets things and admits that he just seems to be forgetful.

There's a lot of ongoing bickering and squabbling between eight-year-old Pauline and eleven-year-old Barry. They tease and taunt and nip and hit each other. There's constant screaming and shouting and running to mother and father with complaints.

Mrs Grant is constantly picking clothes off the floor of the bedrooms and the bathroom – where her children (aged nine to fourteen) have dropped them. Her nagging and scolding about this have little effect.

Aileen has discovered how to get extra attention – the entire mealtime has now become centred around her eating. Her parents coax her to eat and praise her every time she takes a spoonful.

When she comes home in the evening, Alice (15) listens to music on the CD player in the living room. The music is too loud for her father and mother.

CHAPTER 7: TALKING THINGS OUT TOGETHER

There was constant bickering about television in the Spence family (mother, father and three children, aged six to thirteen). The parents were unhappy about the amount of time their children spent watching TV – and about the content of some of the programmes they were watching. The children also squabbled a lot about which programme to watch at a particular time.

After doing a parenting course, Tom and Anne Spence decided to sit down with their children and talk this problem out with them. In that way all the family had an opportunity to state how they saw things, how it affected them and what they would like to see happening. It took them almost forty minutes to go through the four stages for managing problems as in chapter five. Trying to suit everyone and reach agreement was extremely difficult – each one had to compromise and settle for something less than they wanted – but they did manage to reach agreement on a number of issues.
1. No TV without planning – and each child can plan to watch 5 hours a week.
2. No TV after 10.00 p.m. (adult viewing time) unless a parent is present.

3. News, documentaries and educational programmes can be watched at any time in addition to the five hours of TV.

These arrangements would certainly not be appropriate in every family – what suits one family can often prove impossible, even depressing, for another. But the point is that the Spences were able to talk about a difficult area that had been causing tension and conflict – and they managed to reach agreement, with each one having some sense of being involved in the final agreement. They were brave to tackle such a major area of family life. **It is generally better to get some experience and build up skills by starting with minor problems or with planning something enjoyable like an outing or holiday.**

The aim of this course is to build greater respect between family members. Our goal is to help all the members of a family to co-operate in *making* decisions and to live with the results of what they decide. It is the experience of many families that one of the most effective ways of encouraging this is to have a regular, perhaps weekly, time when each family member has a chance to be heard.

In that way, members of a family can involve others in the decisions that affect them.

What is a 'family meeting'?

When parents first hear of family meetings they may react to the idea. "Why can't we just talk things out as they come up?" they ask. "Why go to the bother of a formal set up – it sounds very stilted!" This is a valid objection – it *is* important to learn to deal with problems as they crop up. But there is also a value in having formal meetings. Children often feel more involved at these times, and feel more committed to decisions that are made as a result. Surveys of young people's attitudes show that many of them would love to have the opportunity to express ideas in a calm atmosphere at home.

The idea of the family meeting is not to hand over decision-making to the children but to give them a real say in decisions that affect them. Each one gets a chance to speak, to ask questions, to air grievances, to offer suggestions and to take part in making plans and decisions. Good things that have been happening can also be pointed out and encouraged.

This last point is important. Family meetings are not just about problems and complaints. They can lead to boredom and frustration if we do not make time for encouraging one another and for planning treats, outings and fun.

But why bother?

"Things are okay," some parents will say. "We'll leave well enough alone!" They forget that the old proverb, 'a stitch in time saves nine' applies to family life too. It is easier and more effective to deal with tensions and talk out limits in a relaxed, respectful way instead of trying to cope with the crisis of the moment. Regular time spent talking out chores, bedtimes, coming-in times, television, etc. is time well spent.

In healthy families, limits are never established and sorted out once and for all. What is working well now may not be effective in six months, or in a year. In the last chapter we saw that the key to good discipline is good communication, and regular sit-down sessions with one or more of the children help to keep the lines of communication open. They also **lead to fairer and more peaceful family living, offering children the framework and limits that they both fight against and crave**. A half-hour chat can turn a sense of chaos and depression around and bring back a measure of hope.

Helping to form values

There are other advantages. James and Kathy McGinnis, authors of *Parenting for Peace and Justice*, tell of a married couple they knew who opted for a simpler, more Christian life-style – but did not involve their children in that decision. The children reacted angrily to their parents' decision to buy second hand furniture, "Why should we have to be poorer!" These children are now married and their values seem quite materialistic. James and Kathy, on the other hand, have had family meetings for many years. In their family, some things are *not* open for discussion – like concern for the poor, recycling waste, simpler living – but they discuss and negotiate and compromise on the *ways* in which all this is done. The result is that their children do not seem to resent these things and are developing sound values. Children will form their *own* values, different from ours, but **involving them in making decisions helps them learn to think for themselves, develop conscience and form stronger values.**

You can't just tell children to sort out their own squabbles, and then go off and leave them there. You sometimes need to spend time with them helping them to see how differences can be settled without hitting or kicking or insulting.

DISABILITY AND PARENTING

Do parents of disabled children need a different kind of parenting support? Family Caring Trust believes that they both do and do not. It is sometimes helpful to create 'special interest' groups – of lone parents, of grandparents, of fathers, or of parents of children with a disability – to discuss the special challenges (and joys) that these groups can face.

If we are serious about building genuine community, however, we need to be wary of further isolating people who may already feel isolated from and misunderstood by the rest of the community. Parents are often surprised to discover that a problem they have is shared by other parents in very different circumstances and has nothing to do with their child's disability. Moreover, many of the parenting suggestions in this book – like not doing too much for children and encouraging them to take more responsibility for themselves – are particularly important in dealing with disability. Disabled children have the same need for gentlelove and firmlove as any other child. A balanced approach might be to do a general parenting programme in the community as well as belonging to a monthly 'special interest' support group.

The wider community might also benefit a great deal from more exposure to parents of children with a disability. We might learn to have a greater appreciation of the dignity of these children and the fullness of life that they and their parents can enjoy.

How it works

Family meetings do not have to include the whole family. Many things are best dealt with on a one-to-one basis or in a smaller family grouping – especially matters that are important to one person but of little concern to others. Moreover, **regular sit-down sessions with *individual* members of the family will often be easier and more helpful**. But there will be times when more than two people need to be involved. Parents can learn a lot from running a few of these more formal sessions first, even if they decide to continue only on a one-to-one basis afterwards. Here are some general guidelines for family meetings of three or more people.

The first few family meetings were disastrous. Nobody seemed to want to co-operate and I ended up arguing and scolding. Things improved when I started using the stages for managing problems. When they have no framework, there's chaos – they need certain limits and guidelines.

It helps to meet at the same time every week for a fixed time, perhaps 30-40 minutes (less for younger families). If possible, choose a time when everyone can let go and be fairly relaxed, so not when a favourite TV programme is on!

Some families like to begin by looking over the decisions made at the last meeting and encouraging any progress. Then they ask what anyone wants to talk about and decide which topics to take first, second, and so on. **They may need to remind everyone of the two guidelines:**
1. No interrupting – wait until each person has said all they need to say.
2. All agreements reached remain until the next family meeting.

In dealing with some issues, the steps for solving problems may need to be followed. (We saw in chapter five that people first say how they see the

problem, next they 'brainstorm' and jot down suggestions without any criticism, then they look at the advantages and disadvantages of each suggestion, and finally they make an agreement.)
Writing down any agreements made and putting the page up where everyone can be reminded of them will often help to make them more effective.

Leading the meeting

Let's run quickly through a meeting then. The leader begins by looking at the decisions made at the previous meeting, "How do you all feel about that now?" Next comes the first point to be discussed. The person who wanted to talk about this speaks about it first. The leader then asks, "Anyone else like to say anything about that?" When everyone has had a chance to speak, one at a time, the question can be asked, "Any ideas on how we might solve this problem?" When all suggestions have been made, each one is looked at, "How do you feel about solving it this way?" When a single solution begins to emerge, the leader checks out, "Are we all willing to try this until the next meeting?"

At first, parents might take turns leading meetings, but one of the children can take over running them after some time. The leader needs to:
1. Start and finish the meeting on time.
2. Keep everybody on one topic at a time.
3. Make sure everyone who wishes has a chance to speak on the topic.
4. Show respect for what each one says by encouraging them to speak and by using active listening.
5. Keep 'complainers' positive during brainstorming by asking what they think might be *done* about a problem.
6. Keep a sense of humour!

Parents will obviously need to decide what is *not* for discussion, but it is not necessary for them to keep tight control on a meeting. And it usually helps to encourage the children to make suggestions *first* on any given topic.

Avoiding mistakes

The family meeting can be a way of developing teamwork and co-operation in a family. But the following mistakes can spoil the effect.
1. Choosing a time for meeting that does not suit some of the family.
2. Starting late – or going on too long.
3. Having too much emphasis on complaints and problems.
4. Not keeping to agreements made.
5. One parent not getting into the spirit of the meeting – or taking over.

Some of these mistakes will obviously be made as a family learns the ropes. But the meetings offer great opportunities to practise the skills taught in this course. With practice, they can become part of a whole way of life.

Families at different stages

Meetings for younger children need only last for a short time and might deal with just one topic. Or an alternative to a family meeting for younger children is to have a weekly 'family hour' – a time when parents make a special effort to chat and listen, to read stories, to play games and generally to build good memories for their children. This creates a good atmosphere in a home for starting family meetings at a later stage. Remember that the goal is to communicate more openly and make better connections, so we should not get hung up on doing everything 'like the book says!'

If your children are suspicious of your new approach, you might choose a time when you are eating or working or travelling together to deal with issues needing attention. Consulting and making decisions in an informal way like this can still be very helpful when you are careful to use active listening and not to interrupt.

Those who choose not to attend a more formal meeting (including a father or mother) should not be pressured to attend, but it is only fair to explain to them what will happen, for they may be affected by decisions made at meetings, for example about household chores. Sometimes, these same family members decide to join after a short time.

One-to-one meetings.
When introducing new things into a family, it often works best to start small and move slowly. No need to begin family meetings with a big commitment – better to start on the basis of "Let's try a few family meetings and we'll see how they go." Choose a topic that is interesting or enjoyable for the *children*. Then, after the trial period, you can see if there is a desire to continue to talk things out on a regular basis and how often they might like that.

Our experience is that most families who begin family meetings do not continue to meet as a family on a regular basis. They may find it useful to have an occasional meeting to deal with an issue (like chores) that affects all the family, but most negotiating happens informally on a one-to-one basis in their daily lives. A normal family meeting, then, will not include the whole family. It will be a regular sit-down session with at least *one* of the children to talk through decisions that affect that child. It might take the shape of a brief chat after the 'stand and think' discipline we met in chapter six. Or it may occur when we have pulled out of a heated argument and are ready to sit down at a calmer time to talk out a problem.

At times like these, it usually helps to listen to the needs and feelings of the child and what was going on for them at the time. You might help them to see that they will not always get what they want, especially if they go about it in the wrong way. And you can help them to see the wider picture, including the clash between their own feelings and needs and the feelings and needs of others. It is important in all this that they see you caring and friendly as well as firm.

Indeed, there is no need to wait until there is conflict before having a heart-to-heart talk or a good discussion. Having more meals together – breakfasts, lunches, dinners, or a late-evening supper – will often provide opportunities for more connection. Or you can connect with one of the children as you work together on a project like changing the oil in the car, planting seeds in the garden, baking scones, travelling to a music or swimming lesson together... Your interest and involvement with them around these activities may be enough on its own to prevent or solve problems!

Summary
This chapter, then, is about connecting better and having better discussions with our children. Having family meetings as outlined above is one way (but only one) of getting together to talk on a regular basis – there is no need to wait for a crisis before the talking begins. **What we want to ensure is that each person in the family has the opportunity to speak unhindered and that they are given the respect of being listened to.** And we want to help them see a wider picture as they think about their behaviour and its effect on others.

Sometimes we may want to have a bigger, more formal meeting, but most times we may prefer to talk things out in a twosome or threesome. What is important is that we keep connecting with our children and giving them a say in the decisions that affect them. They *need* us to talk things out and negotiate more with them, particularly as they get older. In this way we will be helping them to develop their conscience and to form values for life.

We had formal family meetings a few years ago after doing the course. Now we don't, but we still find that the methods work for us. They have taught us to talk decisions out and let one person speak at a time and give them a sense of being heard.

GETTING IN TOUCH

Parents used to make all the decisions in a home and children were very definitely expected to do what they were told. Today, some people think the shoe is on the other foot and that children have taken over in many homes. What do **you** think?

1. Who do you think makes the decisions in the average home today – the parents? the children? both? For example, who decides how children spend their time? Whose music is played in the living room? How are the chores divided out and who decides? What other important decisions are made, and who makes them?

2. Who do you think *should* make the decisions?

 # PLANS FOR NEXT WEEK

1. How might you have better 'talking out' chats on a regular basis with at least one child? What might be a suitable weekday/ time/ place? What will you say or do to make it attractive to your children to 'sit and talk'? You may like to write down what you plan to do.

2. Taking time out to talk is also great for a couple. Experts recommend a 'weekly date.' This might be a walk, a meal, a film or a drink together, and a chat to catch up or talk things out. (Lone parents might plan a weekly evening out – or an evening in – with friends.) What might suit you?

Plans..._____

Please read chapter eight of this handbook before the next session

TABLE 7: STAGES OF A FAMILY MEETING

What is important is that you keep *connecting* with your children and giving them a say in the decisions that affect them. Having family meetings as outlined below can set you on the right track for doing this.

1. Before the meeting. Find out what needs to be talked about. Perhaps attach a sheet of paper to the wall of the kitchen and allow anyone who wishes to add topics during the week.

2. The decisions we made. You might begin by looking at the decisions made at the last meeting. "How do we feel about them now?" Encourage any improvements or efforts. Make a note of what anyone is unhappy about – "Should we talk about that now or later?"

3. Down to business. Take the first point to be talked about. "Who wanted to speak about this?" Keep to the point, and let anyone who wishes to speak have a turn. Show understanding and give each a hearing without arguing.

4. Brainstorming. Minor issues can be dealt with briefly, but for important matters, gather ideas (brainstorm). "Any ideas on what we might do for our outing?" No discussion or criticism at this stage – all suggestions can be jotted down.

5. Choosing a solution. Next, look at the suggestions. "How do you feel about these ideas?" or "Which of these suggestions do you like best?" If there is not general agreement, you may need to postpone a decision until the following week and try something out for one week.

6. Making a commitment. Once there is general agreement, get a commitment, "Will we all try this until the next meeting?" "Do we need to work out details about who does what?" (For example, who will prepare food, drinks and games for a family outing?)

7. One topic at a time. Any major issues can be dealt with in this way, but it is best not to run overtime – anything not talked about can be first for discussion next week.

8. Ending with a treat. It can be a good idea to end a family meeting with a special snack or treat. That may build good memories and a stronger family bond. And cards or a board game suited to the ages and interests of the children can be an excellent follow-up to a meeting.

9. Putting decisions into action. Someone might be asked to make a note of any decisions made. This can even be put up on the wall of the kitchen as a reminder. They can be talked about at the start of next week's meeting.

CASE STUDIES

Read the following 'family meeting' (better if four people read the four parts aloud). Then, in groups of three, see if you can pick out an example of: encouragement, 'I' messages, brainstorming, active listening, etc. How do you feel about how the meeting is being run – what seems unusual or different?

FATHER: Well, it's a week since our last meeting and I must say there's been a great improvement. It's nice to get up from the table and not to have to remind anyone about clearing up. So I think the decisions we made about the chores have helped. What about the rest of you? Are you happy with the decisions we made last week?

TIM: I'm not. Some people leave their plates on the table when they've finished, and Sheila takes so long eating that I have all the dishes washed by the time she's finished.

MOTHER: Yes, I noticed that. It makes it harder for you, Tim.

FATHER: Well, any suggestions about how we can solve this problem?

TIM: Sheila could finish her meal at the same time as the others.

SHEILA: Hey, that's not fair. I don't get home from school on time, so I'm late starting.

FATHER: Well, Tim has made one suggestion. Any others? (Pause)

TIM: I think if people forget to clear away their plates, they should wash them themselves.

SHEILA: That's terribly complicated. We'd end up arguing over who didn't clear their plates. I think it should be one person's chore to clear the table.

FATHER: Let me see now – that's three ideas – Sheila finish her meal with the others; wash your own dishes if you're late; or make clearing the table one person's chore. Any more? (Pause). Well, Sheila's not happy with the first two ideas, so do you all think it would be a good idea to make clearing the table someone's chore?

TIM: But whose chore would it be?

SHEILA: Why don't we swap around the chores? If I had to wash the dishes, I wouldn't be keeping anyone back.

FATHER: How would you feel about that, Tim? – if you came off wash-up and cleared the table instead.

TIM: Okay.

FATHER: Right, let's decide that until next week and we'll see how we get on... Now, what's the first point you all wanted to talk about?

SHEILA: Mum wanted to talk about bedtimes.

MOTHER: Yes. I'm not happy about bedtimes. We agreed on ten o'clock for you, Sheila, and nine for you, Tim, but both times are being ignored evening after evening.

TIM: But Mom, nine o'clock is *far* too early. I can't even see the news!

SHEILA: He's right, Mum. Lots of girls in my class don't go to bed until after twelve.

MOTHER: I'm not talking about what other girls do. I just know that your father and I need a bit of time to *breathe* in the evenings, and I need you to respect that.

FATHER: That's important. Your mum and I need a bit of space at the end of the day. So how are we going to solve this?

SHEILA: Go to your room if you want time to breathe! Why should we have to suffer?

FATHER: That's one idea. Any others?

TIM: I wouldn't mind going to bed if I didn't have to put the lights out.

FATHER: Two suggestions. Any more? (Silence).

So what does everyone think of the first suggestion – we go to our room.

MOTHER: You know that wouldn't work. There are lots of things to be done in the evenings. We just need peace and a chance to chat as we're doing them.

FATHER: And the second idea. Keep your bedtimes, but don't put the lights out?

MOTHER: No. I don't want you going about in the morning like zombies for want of sleep.

TIM: (Indignant). Mum, we're not babies!

SHEILA: Ah, come on, Mum!

MOTHER: Well, I don't mind you staying awake a bit later if we don't all have to pay the price for it with your grumpiness in the morning.

FATHER: Looks like the second solution is best then. But how will you work it so you won't be over-tired in the mornings?

TIM: Well, we could put the lights out after an hour.

MOTHER: An hour! No way. Let's see how things work out with half an hour first.

FATHER: But what I'd like to know is – are you going to take *responsibility* for switching off your lights without being *reminded*?

SHEILA: I am.

TIM: I am.

FATHER: Is that a promise – from both of you?

BOTH: Yes.

FATHER: Are you happy with that too, Christine?

MOTHER: Yes, I'll go along with it... But what happens if lights are not out on time?

FATHER: Okay – any ideas on what should happen if lights are not out on time?....

CHAPTER 8: BRINGING IT ALL TOGETHER

Twelve-year-old Sheila had been in a bad mood all morning. She greeted all questions with a grunt or a silent scowl. Eventually she had a run-in with her father and called him a pig. This was unacceptable behaviour, but her father, knowing that it was not the right time to deal with it effectively, refused to take the bait and did the opposite to what Sheila expected. "Oink! Oink!" he replied, playfully mimicking a pig.

It was not a bad approach. A sense of humour is a great help to a parent, and Sheila's father was able to take the heat out of a nasty situation by remembering that. It is important to be flexible in applying the skills in this book.

It is also good to bear in mind that these skills are not just useful for parenting. They can be helpful for our development as persons and will tend to spill over onto our relationships with relatives and other adults.

Settle for less than perfection.
We acquire skills when we practise them regularly. Many of us know from learning to type or to play a musical instrument that we seem to go backwards at times before taking another leap forward. Remembering this may help us to look on the bright side, to see problems as challenges and not to listen to discouragement.

Discouragement and guilt are two great enemies. It is so easy to blame ourselves and think we are responsible for our children's behaviour. We may be tempted to give up when things do not go as planned. Our children may continue to keep their rooms untidy, to make mistakes, to test us in new ways. But what is our goal? Certainly not perfection! Parents who settle for a good deal less than perfection save themselves a lot of frustration and discouragement. We have to remember that **our goal is not to have perfect, well-behaved children right now but to build better, more respectful relationships with them and to support them as they grow in responsibility**.

We do not live in a perfect world. Some days we will feel under the weather and find it hard to cope with anything. Sometimes we will make decisions on the run, with no discussion. Sometimes we will end up letting bedtimes and chores and everything else go by the board because we have too many other things to worry about. That is okay. No one is totally consistent, and it is no harm for your children to see that you are human. Let's look briefly at the main points of the course, then, and try to see them in context.

USEFUL ORGANISATIONS

ALCOHOL The **Alcoholics Anonymous** helpline is 020-7833-0022 **Al Anon** and **Alateen** support friends and relatives of those with drink problems. Tel. 020-7403-0888.

BEREAVEMENT Cruse offers support to anyone who has been bereaved. 0845-585565 **Compassionate Friends** For parents whose child has died. 0117-953-9639

BULLYING Anti-Bullying Campaign Helpline for parents. 020 7378-1446

DRUGS National Helpline is 0808-776600

EATING DISORDERS Eating Disorders Assoc. Their Youth helpline is 01603-765050, and their general helpline is 01603-621414

LESBIAN/ GAY Fflag. Support for lesbian/ gay people and their parents. 020 8467-0309

LESS ABLED Dial UK Helpline for less abled and for their carers 01302-310123

LONE PARENTS Gingerbread 020-7336-8183

PARENTING Family Caring Trust – resources for setting up parenting courses 028-3026-4174 **Parentline** – helpline for parents and step-parents who need someone to talk with 0808-800-2222 **Trust for Study of Adolescence** – 01273-693311.

RAPE For local **Rape Crisis Helplines** check your telephone directory.

SUICIDE/ DESPAIR Papyrus supports parents anxious about children committing suicide. Tel: 01706-214449. **The Samaritans** have a 24-hour Helpline for people in despair 0845-909090

Becoming a responsible parent. Underlying the whole course is the need to see all members of a family as equal. **Parents have special responsibilities and a special leadership role, but each one in the family needs to be treated with respect as a person of equal dignity.** In the past, there was not enough respect for children; they were not equal. Today, it often seems as if things have gone to the opposite extreme and that it is the children who rule the parents. Instead of the consistent firmlove they need, 'discipline' often happens only when they demand attention with a crisis. Instead of gentlelove, we give them expensive gifts, computer games, more television, more treats with their peers – and we expect too little of them. Being slaves to our children, serving them and shielding them from responsibilities is a misunderstanding of true love. This course encourages us to become *responsible* parents rather than that kind of 'good' parent. And that means two things above all – **firmlove** (firmly and consistently applying consequences, involving them in housework, giving 'I' messages…) and **gentlelove** (listening, encouraging, affection, etc.)

Firmlove does not mean a return to past methods. We do not have to decide what our children must wear or control every aspect of their behaviour. That *might* produce the 'correct' behaviour while leaving the child immature, doing the right things for the wrong reasons. **They are much more likely to become responsible when given responsibility, including greater freedom to choose.** This will mean spending time 'connecting' with them, supporting them and training them to choose wisely. When they do choose, we need to allow them to live with the consequences of their choices except when there is danger. In that way they will learn quickly and the burden of discipline will lessen for us.

It would seem to be important, then, to keep a balance between letting go and continuing to be involved. **We cannot just hand over decision-making to children and expect them to make choices entirely on their own. They need some support and guidance** as they gradually grow in their ability to make decisions. They will constantly be learning, of course, from the example of our own lives, observing what we do and say. But they also need to hear what is important to us, what we like and dislike, and what we value – they need feedback on their behaviour in the form of our 'I' messages.

I used to think that all a parent needed was love. Love was the answer. The course has helped me to see that you need skills as well. You know you need skills for nursing or teaching and so on – that love isn't enough – yet you drift into being a parent without any training whatsoever.

Positive Parenting

They also need lots and lots of gentlelove. False praise is not part of that, but children do need us to be interested and encouraging. See if you can cut out all criticism (*personal attack*), and try to postpone most corrections until later. If you keep on the lookout for co-operation, effort and improvement, and you draw attention to these, your children will grow in

confidence and skill. So it helps to be specific in pointing to the good *effects* of what they do, yet doing so in a low-key way, without exaggerating.

Gentlelove also includes affection, touch, caring, making children special and doing fun things with them or taking them on trips that build good memories for them. Part of this is being available when they have problems or strong feelings, but it also means making time for regular chats, asking about the specific details of their lives and listening with genuine interest and attention. In the case of younger children, bedtime may be a good time for these chats; a special supper once a week may be best with older children.

Change comes gradually

Change does not happen overnight – it comes gradually. And it starts with us, not our children. As the ideas in this book seep in, we find ourselves speaking differently or listening differently. And as we change, we find we are no longer rewarding misbehaviour and that there are positive changes in our children.

One of the big changes we may notice in ourselves is that we tend to stand back and think. Faced with challenges like drug use, under-age drinking – or just lack of co-operation and grumpiness – we may find ourselves asking, "What is this child seeking?" or, "Who owns this problem – my child or me?" or "How can I encourage her/him to be more responsible in this situation?" Questions like this can open the way to becoming more effective.

Other changes arise when we have a regular chat with a child or some form of family meeting. Talking things through gives us opportunities to practise using the various skills in this book – listening, managing problems, encouraging, giving responsibility, being more flexible...

In making changes, it helps to be flexible and look for balance – for there is no instant recipe for bringing up children. If applying consequences only gets a child's back up and does not appear to be working in a particular instance, you may need to drop it and try something else – perhaps erring on the side of affection and making better 'connections.'

Where from here?
Finally, a word about where you might like to go from here. The reason why many parents do not change is because they drift along without much thought or reflection, reacting as they have always reacted. Consider taking space at the same time each day – in the morning or after work – to plan for your family, "How can I parent a little better or connect better with my family today?" The best parenting may be at times that are unplanned – being available when a *child* wants to talk or do something rather than when *we* are ready. But sometimes planning helps things to happen, so we *can* make a difference when we plan: "What game or fun thing will I do with a child today?" "Who will I take for a cycle this evening?" "How can I involve a child in a task instead of doing it by myself?" And (not forgetting the priority!) "What would my partner really like me to do today?"

The little boy in the house next to me was driving his mother around the bend. As a result of the course she took control and I saw a transformation in him. That's what made me do the course.

Finding support
Another thing that can help is to read back over a section of this book at a definite time each week. It is hard to take it all in the first time, and you hear things freshly when you dip into the book again. That may help you decide (possibly with a partner) on a new approach to take with a child. **Change is *always* possible.**

It is difficult, however, to keep making the effort to apply new skills without the support of others. Some kind of support group can make a big difference, whether it comes from your extended family, your friends, your faith community, some of the people who did this course with you, or an organisation you trust. Some parents do this course a number of times and claim to get more out of it the second time round. Or you might move on to another course like 'Parenting Teenagers' or 'Parent Assertiveness.'

If things are very tough, you may need to look for more specialised help from your local social services, health visitor or one of the list of organisations in this chapter.

A great deal is at stake. Many of us tend to drift along, not asking ourselves what we really want in life. Perhaps we want a good time, interesting work, money... But few things we do can be as important or rewarding as supporting our children in becoming responsible, caring adults, capable of playing their part in improving society and making our world a more just and peaceful place.

KEEPING A BALANCE

A balanced life is one that makes time for work and play, for exercise and relaxation, for gentlelove and firmlove, for fun and for reflection, for telling your children where you stand as well as for listening to them with understanding. It also includes making space for things as different as fresh air, friendships and a healthy diet.

Time for the spirit
You balance your life, then, not by going along with the crowd but by having more fun, firmness and affection in your family life. Put on some music you like and dance with the children. Encourage them to play music and show an interest in it. Get out into the fresh air with them and expose them as much as possible to natural things – animals, flowers, trees, water, birds, sky, sand – instead of the artificial world of television and computer games. All these things make time for the spirit in children – and in yourself.

You also make time for the spirit when you make time for reflection and for finding a spiritual depth in your own life – your thirst for these things usually rubs off on your children.

Involvement in the community
It will often help to belong to organisations that aim to restore justice and balance to our environment and world. Studies show that this helps children have a more positive outlook on life, especially if you also play a part in helping to build community in your own neighbourhood. Be a community builder. Keep in touch with your extended family, perhaps swapping children for holidays with their aunts and uncles. But maybe in today's world you need to *build* an extended family of your own. If you are on the lookout, you will usually find opportunities. Perhaps it will mean having a more open house, joining a parent-teacher group, running a Charity coffee morning, extending the hand of friendship to an elderly couple but also letting them baby-sit for you on occasions. Anything that introduces more safe adults into your life will probably benefit both you and your children. (Children's connection with adults outside the family has also been shown to be a major factor in lessening their involvement in crime.)

Finding the time for this balance will involve some sacrifices, perhaps less overtime, less money, less television viewing, fewer time-consuming hobbies or obsessions. But the benefits are much greater than the sacrifices.

GETTING IN TOUCH

1. Looking at the last column of Table 8 (the responsible approach), can you find examples there of the following skills:

Applying consequences. Offering choices. Developing responsibility. Giving encouragement. Active listening. Giving 'I' messages. Withdrawing. Brainstorming. Using the four stages of problem-solving.

2. Could you add a ninth problem/challenge to the first column – perhaps one that you meet from your own child? How might you fill in the other columns to match it?

PLANNING AHEAD

1. What single change would you most like to make in yourself or in your family over the next few months? What plans do you need to make to introduce it? What will help you to remember that? You may like to write down your plan.

2. How do you feel about sitting down on your own at a specific time each weekend to plan how you will be a more creative parent in the coming week, foreseeing opportunities to connect with a child – and possibly to deal with a tension? What might be a good day and time?

Plans..._____

TABLE 8: THE RESPONSIBLE APPROACH

Table 8 shows three different approaches parents can take. The responsible approach may mean stopping to ask ourselves, "Who owns this problem?" or "How can I encourage greater responsibility here?"

Problem/ Challenge	Dictator Approach	Permissive Approach	Responsible Approach
1. Child refuses to eat.	Lecture, force, or scold.	Allow child to have own way.	Begin to involve child in planning meals. Use consequences, e.g. "no dessert if dinner is not eaten."
2. Child not working at school.	Stand over child, force, punish, nag.	Bribe child – or ignore completely.	Allow child to take responsibility for own schoolwork, but show interest and encourage improvement/ effort.
3. Child defies parent/ is disobedient.	Threaten. Force.	Coax, apologise, or plead.	It may be best to postpone discussion until child is calmer. Begin with active listening.
4. Child 'forgets' chores.	Remind, scold, demand, nag.	Do the chores yourself.	Discuss it at family meeting and 'brainstorm' on consequences of neglecting chores
5. Child rude to parents in front of visitors.	Make scene, order, humiliate.	Pretend not to notice, plead, bribe.	Give an 'I' message and/or offer your child a choice. Don't worry what your friends think – though they will probably be impressed.
6. Child breaks a window.	Lose temper, humiliate, shout.	"It doesn't matter. We'll fix window."	Stay calm. Ask child (if old enough) to pick up glass. Make arrangements to subtract cost from pocket money.
7. Teenage child refuses to go to church.	Make scene, threaten, insist.	Remind, plead, coax – or just say nothing.	Postpone discussion. Later, use four stages for managing problems, including listening and speaking your own values.
8. Your son is hit by older sister.	Judge. Scold. Punish older sister.	Plead not to hit. Console, "Don't cry."	Use active listening with upset child and ask aggressor, "How will you make up to him?" Allow them settle their own squabbles when possible.
9. A challenge you meet in your own family.			

CASE STUDIES

Two or three people may like to read aloud the conversations below. You might then discuss the questions that follow in groups of three. Can you see ways in which the skills taught in this book can also apply to adults?

Case Study 1

MOTHER: They're your good shoes, Jim – you know you can't go out in the mud in them.

JIM: Ah, mum, the boys are waiting. You always spoil my fun.

DAD: I can't see why he can't go out in those shoes. They'll do okay. Let him run on.

MOTHER: Well, I'm the one who has to clean the mud off the carpet when he doesn't change. Are you prepared to do that if he comes back in with muddy shoes?

DAD: Mm, I suppose you have a point. Okay, you better change your shoes.

What usually happens in a case like this? What skills is the mother using? What do you think of her approach?

Case Study 2

Five-year-old Catherine has scarcely touched her dinner but wants to have her pudding. Her father explains that she doesn't have to eat her dinner if she doesn't want to, but she can't have pudding if she doesn't eat it. Granny has been listening, and now interrupts:

GRANNY: Of course the child can have her pudding, Gerry. I didn't starve you when you were a child. Here's your pudding, dear – and just enjoy it.... I never heard such nonsense!

FATHER: I appreciate your kindness to Catherine, Mom. But I don't want her to develop bad eating habits, and I feel upset and discouraged when you give in to her like this.

What usually happens in a situation like this? What skills is the father using? He may not get granny to change, of course, but what are the advantages of this approach?

Case Study 3

Mr West used to shout, nag, and scold to get his 15-year-old daughter, Sandra, out to school. Since doing this course, however, he is encouraging her to take more responsibility for herself in the mornings. The result is that she is often late for school. Mr West believes that she should face the consequences of being late, but one evening Sandra's teacher happens to meet him.

TEACHER: Oh, Mr West, could I have a word with you? It's about Sandra. I'm sorry to have to tell you she's been late to school almost every day for the past two weeks. I wonder could you make sure she gets in on time in future.

MR WEST: Thank you for mentioning this. That must be very annoying for you to have Sandra come in late when you're trying to get things done.

TEACHER: It certainly is. You'll have to do something about it.

MR WEST: Have you spoken to Sandra about this yourself?

TEACHER: Oh yes. But it doesn't seem to have made any difference.

MR WEST: I see. That makes it more difficult, doesn't it? And what do you usually do with a child who doesn't behave?

TEACHER: Well, I sometimes speak to the parents... Or I send her to the principal.

MR WEST: Well, thanks for speaking to me, Miss Wright: I've told Sandra I want her to take responsibility for getting to school on time, and I want you to feel perfectly free to deal with her in the usual way. It might do her no harm to have to face the principal.

What usually happens in a case like this? What skills is Mr. Walsh using? How do you feel about his approach?

Appendix: What is 'Spiritual' for a Family?

The search for 'more'

Many of us drift along in life, doing good things, coping with work and family, but almost too pressured and busy to make room in our lives for something 'spiritual.' Then something happens – a crisis, the death of someone close, personal suffering – or we read an article that stops us in our tracks. We may realise then that a part of us is dissatisfied, not fulfilled, restless, and we begin to search for the spiritual, for the 'more' that is missing.

What is offered to families in this quest for meaning is often unsuitable. So here is something to try. Read through the list of things at the end of this appendix (page 74). They are all things that help *some* families to be 'spiritual' *some of the time*. Tick any ideas that you think might be spiritual things to do in your home, given your circumstances:

Many different ways

Maybe your first reaction to this list is that there are things in it that you do not find helpful, that you may even find painful. If you're a single parent, for example, mention of things that couples might do may not help. If you do not have children, mention of parenting may be painful. In other words, what some people find helpful in building their family life may be discouraging or depressing for others. It obviously makes sense to have some balance between gentlelove and firmlove, between activity and reflection, but that said, **there is not just one way for a family to be spiritual. There are as many different kinds of family spirituality as there are families.**

Different styles, different circumstances

Sadly, what some faith communities offered families in the past did not allow for different styles and circumstances. They failed to see that what is a wonderful celebration for one family may feel like chaos – or too much alcohol – for another. One family may deal with tensions by sitting down to talk things out after a row, another family may shout and scream – and normal life resumes when one person merely clears their throat in a particular way that lets everyone know the row is over. Sexual intercourse may be vitally important for one couple's closeness: for another couple 'making love' may mean being intimate with no question of sexual intercourse. Then there are things like family prayer that may work well in one family, and the very mention of it may start World War Three in another family – where the only prayer may be a silent one of blind faith and trust in a parent's heart. Another area of difference is family meals. Quite a few families never have dinner around a table. Some of them don't even have a table, and asking them to eat at a table not only doesn't work but can make them feel bad, disheartened, the opposite of affirmed. Their time to talk over food may be over a bite of supper in the living room – or over take-away food and a few beers! And who is to say that a meal in a fast-food restaurant 'doesn't count'? Holiness is flexible because love takes many shapes.

Picnics and fun

A second thing that may have struck you in the list below is that it included things like teaching children to ride bikes. What was offered in the past as family spirituality tended to be too *limited*. The emphasis was on prayers and religious practices, with recommendations on being patient, forgiving one another and so on. Having picnics, involving children in doing chores or having fun with them had nothing to do with that. They were okay things to do, but they were secular, not part of spirituality, not something encouraged in sermons or homilies.

It is not just that these things were not encouraged: faith communities often recommended families to set *aside* the details of their ordinary, messy, daily lives in order to find God. But setting those details aside missed the point. For it is there above all that we have to find God. That is where we love or fail to love. And **love is the basic sign of spirituality. If it is missing, that is a sure sign that our spirituality is mistaken.**

That does not mean that prayer and religious practices do not have an important part to play. Of course they help. But working at family relationships is the *foundation* of family spirituality, and an emphasis on prayer is misguided except in the context of daily living and loving.

Love in the midst of the hassle

Family spirituality, then, is in the daily hassle of family life, in the methods of parenting taught in this book, in the tears and laughter and sweat of daily living, in the cooking and cleaning, in listening and caring and touching, in talking out tensions, celebrating, telling stories, having fun... Daily living is where love is tested and grows weaker or stronger.

The love we are talking about here is not a feeling. There may or may not be loving feelings. But loving is not easy. There are few people so difficult to love as the members of our own families. Loving them demands self-sacrifice. It means pulling myself out of my comfort zone for the sake of another. Obviously, that does not mean doing everything for my children and being their doormat, though that is how some religious people have thought about love in the past. That is bad religion and mistaken spirituality. Genuine love, however, is what family spirituality is all about. For God is love, and wherever love is, God is there.

Noticing God

The problem is that we don't notice God. Most families do hundreds of caring and thoughtful things for each other every day, but they don't see God in them. They have been conditioned to think that the only way to experience God is in prayer. That is monastic spirituality – withdrawing from the world to seek God in religious rituals, prayer, etc. It

misses God in the ordinariness of family life. We fail to see that God is there all the time in loving acts in our own home. Remember, wherever love is, God is. What families need is not so much to do more 'spiritual' things as to become aware of how spiritual the things they are doing already are – and perhaps to do them with more love.

*I didn't like my work taking me away from my son, so I told him that Saturday mornings would be just for him from then on, and that I would do whatever **he** wanted me to do on those mornings. So what did he want me to do first? Cycle seven miles to the seaside and have a picnic there! Now, this was December, and I hadn't been on a bike for over ten years! But I got the bikes fixed up during the week, and we headed off on a cold, drizzly morning, and we ate our sandwiches in the rain. And you know something? That's fifteen years ago, and he has left home now, but he told me recently that that is one of his best childhood memories! I didn't know that I was 'doing family spirituality' at the time.*

But how do we experience God in daily family living? That is an important question.

It is also a new question that has been very little explored, for family spirituality is a new field. Recently, we have been asking friends to think about it, and here, for example, is what one man told us. He is someone who goes off to a corner of the house to pray for fifteen minutes every day, and on this occasion he was praying to be open to whatever God had in store for him. His wife came in and told him she had a cramp across her shoulders. "Sit down," he said, "and I'll try massaging your shoulders." Ten minutes or so later, the pain had eased and she left. He settled back to pray. Then his eight-year-old daughter burst in, "Dad, come quick," she said, "There's a daddy-long-legs in the bedroom and I'm scared of it." Dealing with it took quite a while because he had to help it escape out the window and not kill it. Eventually he got back to pray to find that his half-hour had nearly run out. But here is the point of the story. "A year ago," this man said, "I would have felt angry and frustrated that I wasn't getting any peace to pray. But here I was getting a very clear message from God that I was praying when I was massaging my wife's shoulders and I was praying when I was responding to my daughter's fears. God is teaching me," he said, "that meeting interruptions with love during prayer-time is an even better prayer – in fact, God is teaching me that meeting interruptions with love at *any* time is a prayer. Because God is present whenever there is love – and maybe especially in the interruptions."

Satisfying their thirst

A mother also told us about settling her son to bed. She had read him a story and put out the light when he said. "Mum, I'm thirsty."

Now, she knew he was probably just playing for time but she explained, "Something clicked with me at that moment, 'If you give a drink of water in my name...' And I went and got him the water."

Can you see the difference awareness makes? If we are serious about spirituality in our families, doing traditionally 'holy' or 'devotional' things may be missing the point unless we are allowing God into the family through our loving. If I am too busy doing good things for my family and haven't time to talk to my daughter when she wants to talk, I may be tuning God out.

Summing up

To sum up, then. For many centuries, what has been presented to families as 'spiritual' has been selling them short in that it was too rigid and too limited. Family spirituality is flexible; it takes as many shapes as there are families. Its sign is love. Not the *feeling* of love, but love in the daily hassle of family life, in dealing with the moans and complaints, the bickering and the tensions of daily living as well as in affection and fun and celebration. That is where God is.

From time to time you may like to look back through the list of things below that help to build family spirituality. Each time, you might highlight one or two areas where you would like to restore the balance a little in building your own family life.

Good luck with that. We would be delighted to hear from you at any time about 'God moments' in your own family when you have experienced God, not by *withdrawing* from the daily hassle but by getting involved in it with love.

We would like to acknowledge the influence and help of the following people in writing this appendix:
Mary Cunningham, Jack Dominian, David Gamble, Philip Leonard, Finbarr Lynch, and David Thomas.

APPENDIX (continued)

Below are some things that can be spiritual for a family. Tick anything that you think, given your circumstances, might be spiritual (or holy) for you or your family.

- **Teaching the children to ride bikes.**
- **Being affectionate, warm, gentle or good-humoured with members of your family.**
- **Firmly applying consequences to children's misbehaviour.**
- **Having a daily, uninterrupted 'space' with your partner for 10-15 minutes.**
- **Taking time to plan the weekend with family in mind.**
- **Praying with the children at bedtime.**
- **Joining them for supper even though you don't want to eat.**
- **Telling them your memories of them as children, and of yourself as a child.**
- **Having a picnic or a barbecue.**
- **Keeping up connections with your own parents, siblings and relatives.**
- **Attending church, synagogue or mosque together.**
- **Making love.**
- **Being part of a local support group of families.**
- **Telling bedtime stories (sometimes Bible/Koran stories) and having bedtime chats.**
- **Play-wrestling on the floor.**
- **Having some religious practices in the home, e.g., at different seasons of the year.**
- **Playing games with family members.**
- **Telling family members, within reason, what you think and feel.**
- **Being available when a family member wants to talk or to play.**
- **Making up after a row.**

- **Praying before meals.**
- **Slowing down to involve a child in doing work with you.**
- **Celebrating birthdays, anniversaries special occasions, family traditions.**
- **Reading and praying on the scriptures of your faith community.**
- **Training and involving children in doing household chores.**
- **Watching TV or a video together.**
- **Caring for people in need – or doing other voluntary work in your community.**
- **Knowing the details of your children's lives and asking about them.**
- **Praying as a couple.**
- **Helping children to organise their time.**
- **Taking 'space' and doing things *you* enjoy to renew yourself for your family.**
- **Chatting over meals together.**
- **Making time for your own personal prayer and spiritual development.**
- **Finding books to stretch a child (and to stretch yourself!).**
- **Having a weekly 'date' with your partner.**
- **Befriending an elderly couple – and perhaps having them baby-sit for you.**
- **Facing up to and talking out tensions.**
- **Enjoying Nature together.**
- **Taking regular 'planning time' to plan to do some of the things above.**

FURTHER READING

*In writing this book, we have attempted to produce something short, simple and practical. For those who want more, there are many good books on parenting. Here are just a few. Some of them, perhaps, take too rigid, or too democratic an approach. The authors prefer to see more emphasis on parental affection, example and guidance, with a **gradual** handing over of responsibilities to a child. That said, there is a great deal to recommend in these books.*

The Secret of Happy Children (ISBN 9 780722 536698) Also **More Secrets of Happy Children (ISBN 9 780722 536704).** Steve Biddulph writes with humour and simplicity – these are inspiring and challenging books for parents. Publ. Thorsons.

The Effective Parent, by Dinkmeyer and McKay. Could be more simply written, but has a wealth of sensible ideas and good examples. Publ. AGS, Circle Pines, Minnesota. ISBN 0-913476-68-4 **The Parent's Guide,** from the same authors and publisher looks at the special challenges provided by teenagers. ISBN 0-913476-82-X

Children: The Challenge, by Rudolf Dreikurs and Vicki Soltz. A classic best seller, helpful on how parents can allow children learn from the consequences of their behaviour. Publ. Plume/Penguin. ISBN 0-88671-356-0

Parent Effectiveness Training, by Dr Thomas Gordon. A classic book for parents that is particularly good on active listening, I-messages, and problem solving. Publ. Penguin Putnam Inc ISBN 04522646.

The Heart of Parenting, by John Gottman. The findings of one of the leading research psychologists are made available here in simple language. You will see how the 5-15s Programme reinforces what Gottman calls 'emotional coaching' - how parents speak, listen, encourage, show affection, respect feelings, offer choices and allow children to learn from the consequences of their choices. Publ. Bloomsbury, ISBN 0-7475-3312-1

Nurturing Good Children Now by Ron Taffel. A fresh, well-researched book from a family therapist who has sounded the alarm about the effects on children of the pop-culture and their 'second family' of peers. Golden Books 1999 ISBN 1-58238-009-0.

Two general background books to help understand the family are:

Families and how to survive them, by Robin Skynner and John Cleese. Publ. Methuen ISBN 0-413-69600-6

The New Peoplemaking, by Virginia Satir. for parents who wish to understand what is happening between family members. Offers hope for changing destructive family patterns. Publ. Science and Behaviour Books, California, ISBN 0-8314-0070-6

SUPPORT FOR PARENTING

THE 'NOUGHTS TO SIXES' PARENTING PROGRAMME

Seven or eight weekly sessions offering effective parenting support to parents of babies, toddlers, pre-schoolers or children in the first few years of primary school. Simply written, jargon-free, common sense approach. Produced in co-operation with Barnardos. The boxed kit includes a video (incorporating the BBC's acclaimed QED programme on parenting), two leader's guides, twenty-five certificates, and one copy of the parent's handbook, **From Pram to Primary School.**

THE 'FIVES TO FIFTEENS' PARENTING PROGRAMME

Eight weekly sessions to help parents of children five to fifteen years old to improve their communication skills and create a framework of discipline and respect in their families. The boxed kit includes a video (about ten minutes' input for each session), two leader's guides, twenty-five certificates, and one copy of the parent's handbook, **What Can A Parent Do?**

THE 'PARENTING TEENAGERS' PROGRAMME

Six to eight weekly sessions to reinforce the same parenting skills while dealing with the more difficult situations met in the teen years. Because it is so important to reinforce skills being learnt, it is recommended that parents of teenagers experience the Fives to Fifteens programme first, though this is not essential. The kit includes a video, two leader's guides, twenty-five certificates, and one copy of the parent's handbook, **What Can The Parent Of A Teenager Do?**

THE 'PARENT ASSERTIVENESS' PROGRAMME

Seven weekly sessions learning basic assertive skills applied to the workplace or neighbourhood, but especially to family situations. A good way of complementing what has been learnt in the other parenting programmes. Produced in co-operation with Barnardos. The boxed kit includes two leader's guides, a video and one copy of the participant's handbook, **Being Assertive.**

THE 'PARENTING AND SEX' PROGRAMME

Five weekly sessions to help parents learn skills for talking, and getting children talking, about sex (parents are often overlooked in the sex-education process that targets schools and youth clubs). Preferably for parents of primary school children, but it also looks at areas like dating, television viewing, peer pressure... The kit consists of two leader's guides and a copy of the parent's handbook, **Parenting and Sex.**

SUPPORT FOR YOUNG ADULTS

THE YOUNG ADULT ASSERTIVENESS PROGRAMME

Eight weekly sessions to help young adults, aged fifteen and upwards, to learn the same respectful skills as their parents and thus reinforce change within the family system. The emphasis is on growth in self-confidence, saying 'no' to peer pressure and finding fairer, less aggressive ways of dealing with problems. The boxed kit includes a video, two leader's guides, a pack of twenty-five certs, and one copy of the participant's handbook, **Taking Charge of your Life.**

SUPPORT FOR COUPLES

THE 'GROWING IN LOVE' PROGRAMME

Four weekly sessions for groups of women (or of men) *without* their partners. One encouraging effect is that many men (who have not attended a course) experience the *effects* and become more open to experiencing a course for couples (also provided for in the kit). The boxed kit includes two audiotapes, two leader's guides (one for running single-sex groups, and one for running groups of couples), and one copy of the participant's handbook, **Growing in Love.**

THE 'COUPLE ALIVE' PROGRAMME

Six weekly sessions for couples at all stages - engaged, cohabiting, recently married or married up to forty years. Helps couples deepen or renew their love, commitment and understanding for one another. Also teaches the "Listen and Check" method which has reduced rates of separation, divorce and domestic violence in Europe and the United States. The boxed kit includes a video, two leader's guides, and a participant's handbook, **Couple Alive.**

The Trust has no links with any religious body, but there is an optional Christian dimension and an optional Islamic dimension for each course, written by people committed to those faiths.

ADDITIONAL RESOURCES

Manual for training people to run Family Caring Trust programmes. A resource to provide an accredited training for facilitators of parenting programmes (accreditation by the Open College Network at Level 3). Developed by Hallam Caring Services in co-operation with people from the Education, Health, Social Services and Voluntary sectors.

Introductory video 25-min. videocassette useful for information evening/introductory session. Shows effect of parenting course on two families. Made independently by RTE, and provided at duplication cost.

Leader's tape. Audiotape to help facilitators understand their role and to reinforce skills they need.

The Family Dinner Game. For families with pre-teen children. Nurtures communication, fun and emotional support over a weekly family meal. Enthusiastic feedback from families and media.

For over a decade, Family Caring Trust has been the main provider of parent education in the UK and in Ireland. Over a third of a million parents in these isles have taken one of the Trust's courses. The materials have also been adapted to different cultures and translated into Arabic, Czech, Danish, Icelandic, Japanese, Latvian, Russian, Spanish and Welsh. In addition to being widely used by social services and well over a thousand schools and adult education bodies, they have been adopted or endorsed by the following organisations:

The Health Visitors' Association (CPHVA), Barnardos, NCH, The Children's Society, Homestart, The National Childbirth Trust, All the mainstream Christian Churches, NSPCC, Mothers' Union, The Marriage Enrichment Association, and the Psychological Services in Scotland. (Barnardos and the Department of Health have also contributed to the development and production of some of the courses.)

MAKING AGREEMENTS

At the beginning of a course, it may help to discuss and agree on the following guidelines and any other points parents wish to raise.

1. Take it seriously. People generally find this course enjoyable, but you are also asked to take it seriously. It is important, for example, to come to all eight meetings and to practise the skills in between sessions, for each session builds on the one before it. Those who work hard at the skills between sessions tend to see a great improvement in themselves and in their children.

2. Play your part. Some people are naturally shy and reluctant to speak, even in a small group. No one at any stage *has* to talk in the group, but talking things out together can help both you and the others, so the more open you can be the better.

3. Give the others a chance. This guideline is for the person who tends to talk too much. Please don't speak a second time about a topic until everyone has at least had an opportunity to speak once. Hogging the conversation is just not fair to the others. If you tend to overtalk, try going out of your way to draw others out and to encourage them to talk first.

4. Respect people's confidences: During the course, it may happen that members of the group will trust you by telling you personal things about their children. If so, it is important to respect that trust and not to talk about such matters outside the group, because things can sound quite different when they are spoken about out of context.

5. Take it slowly. Don't let discouragement beat you if you make mistakes or seem to be slow about getting results. Learning new skills takes time and patience - you know what it's like learning to cook, to ride a bike, to type, or to play a musical instrument. 'Little and often' is the golden rule for picking up new skills - taking on only a little at a time but practising it often.

6. What works for you. You're not expected to use or to agree with everything on this course. Many parents are already doing a very good job and are not using all these methods - we're all different. But you are asked to give new ideas a fair chance by trying them out - that's the only way to find out what *might* work for you.

7. What works for others. We have just seen that you have a right to be different. You are asked to respect that difference in *others* too. People have a right to their own approach and their own opinion. What works for you may not work for them, so do share with others what works for you, but please do not offer them advice - it is just not helpful to tell others in the group what you think *they* ought to do. In the same spirit of respect, the group leaders will not offer advice either.

8. Look out for strengths. Please do not use the group to make little of your children or to criticise others. Keep on the lookout for strengths and improvements, for this is a positive, family-building support group. It is also a basic principle of the course that to be effective I need to begin by changing *myself*; my children will begin to change when I do.

9. No preaching. The input for this course comes from the leader's guide and video, so the leader will not be giving you advice. Please show the same respect to each other - make suggestions or say what works for *you* but do not tell others what to do. This applies also to a partner who is not doing the course with you, though you might share the book with them.